PRAYING
FOLLOWING
WITH THE
JESUS
CHURCH
DAILY, HOURLY, TODAY

SCOT McKNIGHT

Author of: *The Jesus Creed: Loving God, Loving Others*
and *Embracing Grace: A Gospel for All of Us*

PARACLETE PRESS
BREWSTER, MASSACHUSETTS

Praying with the Church: Following Jesus, Daily, Hourly, Today

2006   First Printing

ISBN 1-55725-481-8

Scripture quotations are taken from the New Revised Standard Version of the Bible, copyright 1989, Division of Christian Education of the National Council of the Churches of Christ in the United States of America. Used by permission. All rights reserved.

Library of Congress Cataloging-in-Publication Data
McKnight, Scot.
Praying with the church : following Jesus daily, hourly, today
  by Scot McKnight.
     p. cm.
  ISBN 1-55725-481-8
  1. Prayer—Christianity. I. Title.
  BV210.3.M38 2006
  248.3'2—dc22   2006002085

10 9 8 7 6 5 4 3 2 1

Published by Paraclete Press
Brewster, Massachusetts
www.paracletepress.com

Printed in the United States of America

TABLE OF CONTENTS

III

CONCLUSION

*For my students who are now laboring
in churches throughout the world
praying and teaching others to pray—
students who are
too numerous to name,
too selfless to notice.*

The aim of man's life is union (henosis) with God.

*This participation takes man within the life of the three
Divine Persons themselves,
in the incessant circulation and overflowing of love
which courses between the Father, the Son and the Spirit,
and which expresses the very nature of God.
Here is the true and eternal bliss of man.*

*Union with God is the perfect fulfillment of the "kingdom"
announced by the Gospel,
and of that charity or love
which sums up all the Law and the Prophets.
Only in union with the life of the Three Persons
is man enabled to love God
with his whole heart, soul, and mind,
and his neighbour as himself.*

A Monk of the Eastern Church

FOREWORD

From their earliest moments, the three monotheistic faiths of Abraham—Judaism, Christianity, and Islam—have all shared certain common assumptions about, and disciplines of, religious and spiritual formation. All three appoint one day each week as sacred unto God. All three require tithing. Each encourages spiritual pilgrimage. All three govern themselves according to the rhythms of a liturgical year; and each teaches the uses of fasting at appointed seasons in either the cycles of physical time or of a believer's individual courses. Most significantly for our purposes here, however, all three have, from their very inception, assumed the practice of fixed-hour prayer as part and parcel of the observant life.

It was understood, that is, that at set hours of each day the faithful would interrupt the business of vocational life in order to praise and worship the Almighty One, thereby not only offering an appropriate sacrifice of time and deliberate intention, but also assuring that the thoughts and actions of each worshiper had been returned to the Source from which he or she had come and to which he or she would ultimately be accountable. In general, the appointed prayers were usually offered in the physical presence of other worshipers, whether family or co-workers or simply co-religionists; but one did not have to be in the physical company of other believers to do so. Because the hours of prayer were fixed or set, one could stop wherever one was, be it alone or in company, and offer the appointed words of praise and thanksgiving, knowing thereby that one was part of the whole company of believers worshiping together across geography and circumstance before the throne of God.

This is a potent image and a potent practice that hones the soul as surely as it hones and shapes the communion of which the soul is a member. It is still assumed today in both Judaism and Islam; in those faiths, the faithful stop and the faithful pray. It was also assumed in apostolic Christianity: Peter received the vision of the descending sheet while on the rooftop in Joppa for noon prayers. The flames of Pentecost descended on the early believers while they were gathered together in an upper room for nine o'clock prayers. Peter and John exercised the first healing after Christ's resurrection by ministering to the cripple whom they found on the Temple steps as they made their way to three o'clock prayers. . . .

Fixed-hour prayer was assumed as part of Christian devotion for several centuries, in fact, until Rome fell. After that, the decimation of Roman civilization drove the dangerous and literate business of fixed-hour prayer into the safekeeping primarily of monasteries and, to some extent, of royal households. Because of those long, dark centuries when only the clergy and the privileged had both prayer books and the literacy with which to use them, fixed-hour prayer (or the keeping of the offices, to use another familiar name for the discipline as it is followed in Christianity) came to be associated in the minds of the humble faithful as particular not to the Christian tradition itself, but to chanting monks and/or times of sequestered individual devotion. Nothing could have been, or could be, farther from the truth. And little could have been more detrimental, more enervating, to the whole body of Christ on earth than the loss of those diurnal rhythms of praise and thanksgiving by all believers. As a result and as a part of its own emergence and re-configuration, what post-modern, post-denominational, post-Reformation Christianity now calls us to is the reclamation by all Christians of fixed-hour prayer and of the spiritual richness that comes from this most ancient and holy practice.

You will read here about several manuals or books for keeping the hours as twenty-first-century Christians. Among them you will discover a chapter about *The Divine Hours*, a manual or breviary that I had the great joy of compiling. But this book is not about any particular prayer book or prayer tool. Rather it is about the fact that now, because primarily of the work of a rising generation of young Christians who want more of the authentic in their Christian practice, there are manifold such books and tools. Scot McKnight, in fact, lovingly introduces some half dozen or so of them. These pages celebrate something else as well, though. They celebrate the fact that in this newfound multiplicity of resources, the individual Christian can experience the freedom of growing from the simpler manuals to the more intricate and sometimes richer ones. This book celebrates, in other words, the near-miracle that one is able now to grow in this discipline in concord with one's own increasing spiritual perception of the place that is prayer.

But this book is more even than all that. This book is the tool that those of us who have worked these fields for many years have not, up until now, had. This book has the power of succinct statement. In one phrase, Scot McKnight has captured the essence of what fixed-hour prayer is: It is praying *with* the Church. What a simple insight, yet brilliant in its perfect accuracy. McKnight has also, pastorally and with great skill, separated the discipline of fixed-hour prayer from the exercise of other forms of prayer, showing us with the deft insights of one who is himself a practitioner, the need for all of them and the place of each way in approaching God.

If a generation of new Christians has opened the doors to fixed-hour prayer, then just as surely Scot McKnight has swept clean the room and prepared a place for all of us to be Church here, undivided and indivisible. I welcome that with quiet joy, and I strongly suspect you will too.

Phyllis Tickle
compiler, *The Divine Hours*
The Farm In Lucy

1

PRAYING *WITH* THE CHURCH

ost Christians are not happy with their prayer life—they either don't pray often enough or well enough. This book is written to help such Christians—and for those who do pray often, this book might also bring a welcoming word.

For far too many Christians the only kind of prayer experience is praying alone *in* the church. This happens whenever an individual prays exactly and only what is on his or her heart. I call this praying *in* the church. Many Christians today, however, are turning to another kind of prayer and rediscovering its formative influences. This second form of prayer consists of set prayers that the Church has written down and prayed for centuries. The Church has always prayed at fixed times with set prayers, and in so praying it creates a sacred rhythm of prayer. I call this praying *with* the Church. When Christians pray at fixed times with set prayers, they join millions of Christians scattered across the globe who routinely pause two or three or even more times in a day to pray what other Christians are praying.

Christians use various terms for praying *with* the Church, such as liturgical prayer, fixed-hour prayers, the Divine

Office, the divine hours, the hours of prayer, or the *Opus Dei* ("the work of God"). No matter what term we use, it is what we are doing that is important: We are joining hands and hearts with millions of other Christians to say the same thing at the same time. By doing this, we are creating in our lives a sacred rhythm of prayer.

A growing number of Christians today are adjusting their lives in order to pray set prayers at fixed times. I stand with them. And when I mention that I practice fixed-hour prayer in public settings, someone nearly always replies, "I've learned to do the same thing, and I love it!"

What may surprise some is that nearly everyone who practices a sacred rhythm of praying finds it life-shaping. As one of my blog readers said in a comment, it takes "the earthbound and frames it in the divine."

I was challenged toward fixed prayers reading Lauren Winner's Girl Meets God *and* Mudhouse Sabbath. *She wrote about prayer in a way that brought depth and a rhythm to faith I felt was missing from my experience. Lauren recommended* The Divine Hours *to me, and I have been very grateful. . . . [I]t helps to bring focus to the daily routine in which it is so easy to become distracted and earthbound. Focusing for a few minutes on the richness of the psalms, historical prayers, and hymns takes the earthbound and frames it in the divine.* —MARK PERRY

BUT NOT IN MY CHURCH

I grew up in a church that did not teach fixed-hour prayer rhythms. We did not pray *with* the Church. Instead, we prayed *in* the church. We were good at it. More than a hundred from our congregation would gather nearly every Wednesday night just for prayer—no sermon, no music just prayer. And many of us (by my count) prayed at home alone and with our families. We were good at spontaneous prayers—at praying what we sensed should be said when we sensed we needed to pray. We prayed alone or together *in* the church.

Let me emphasize that I'm not saying there is anything wrong with praying spontaneous prayers *in* the church. But there is another kind of prayer, taught in the Bible and practiced throughout the history of the Church, that can have a powerful impact on our spiritual life.

Again, let me go back to my experience: I do not recall ever reciting the Lord's Prayer aloud in my church on a Sunday morning or a Sunday evening, or even during the Wednesday evening prayer meeting. Using someone else's prayers was not permissible. (Even Jesus' prayer!) The unwritten code was this: "Do not pray other peoples' prayers." They could endanger one's soul.

I do not mean to be disrespectful here. And I don't recall anyone screeching someone's prayer to a halt or gasping when someone trotted out a line or two from a written prayer, but the word was out and worked itself all the way through our proud church: You can catch spiritual infections from set prayers.

3

We believed, and I joined in with this conviction for a long time, that there was a spiritually dangerous connection between set prayers and impersonal faith. (We did, however, have a choir led by my mother that sang "The Lord bless you and keep you. . . ." nearly every Sunday—and I still like that song because of its constancy.) But the repetition of prayers or especially the reading of the prayers of others was not practiced.

We were given this diagnosis for an argument: *Repetition* leads to *recitation*, and recitation leads to *vain repetitions*. (And we all knew where vain repetitions lead you—right into Dante's *Inferno*, though we didn't read Dante or use any version of his word "inferno.") Before long, we thought, we'd just be mouthing words and not meaning them at all. It is better, we were taught, to say something clumsy but really mean it from the heart than say something profound and poetic and run the risk of not meaning it. If meaninglessness meant vain repetition and meaningfulness meant spontaneous prayers, I would choose the second every time.

But these are not the only two options.

The Bible, Jesus, and the Church teach that we can learn to use set prayers at set times and pray *with* the Church and mean every word we say and, as a result, grow both personally and as a community of faith. So the aim of this book is to encourage Christians to pray not only *in* the church but also *with* the Church.

◆

For most of my life I only prayed extemporaneously. Three years ago, I began praying the offices: morning and evening on a daily basis, midday and compline less frequently. For the past two years, I have exclusively used Northumbria's Celtic Daily Prayer, *and am often amazed by how personally relevant and challenging the prayers and readings have been. Admittedly, I did not expect this, but am so grateful to God for leading me in this direction. The rhythm and relevancy have deepened my prayer life significantly.* —CHRIS MONROE

Praying *with* the Church at fixed times with set prayers can engage the mind, the heart, the soul, and the body— and can be just what prayer was meant to be: the total engagement of the whole church with God.

BUT WHAT ABOUT . . . ?

There was a reason my spiritual mentors frowned upon rote prayers at set times: They knew folks who said fixed-hour prayers and didn't mean them. Let's start right here—humans have a knack for turning religious acts into meaninglessness. But saying the right things is not the point. The point is to learn to engage with God—and the point is also learning to engage with God *together,* not only alone *in* the church but also *with* the Church. Every scene of heaven in the Bible shows us a vision of the Church praying together and singing together and praising together.

"When we pray, we add our own voices to this ceaseless chorus, taking our part in the song that has been sung since creation began. Prayer is the way by which we join earth's refrain to heaven's hymn."

—THE LITTLE BOOK OF HOURS, IX.

But still, no one can dispute the tendency for fixed-hour prayers to slip into mindless, memorized mouthing of words. Whose fault, we need to ask, is that?

If our prayers have become vain repetitions, it is because our heart is not engaged, not because of what we say. I know from personal experience that set prayers have stimulated my own prayers and my own life. For many of us, fixed times for prayer, when, instead of trying to figure out something to say, we say what the Church is saying, might just be the stimulus our prayer life needs. The development of sacred rhythms might help set loose a church that learns to pray together. That is my (spontaneous) prayer for this book.

What we need then is both lively, spontaneous prayers *in* the church and heartfelt prayers *with* the Church. We needn't choose one or the other, nor need we downgrade one or the other. We need both.

AND THIS ALSO . . .

If you compare the written prayers from the psalms, the Lord's Prayer, or those we find in the prayer books of the church, one thing will immediately strike any reader: The prayers from those sources are theologically rich and aesthetically appropriate. I cannot always say this of the spontaneous prayers of many Christians—and I am not impugning their motives or questioning their hearts.

What I *am* suggesting is that spending time with the psalms, the Lord's Prayer, and the prayer books of the church can improve the prayer life of Christians and the church. Time spent with the prayers of others can teach us to pray both alone *in* the church and together *with* the Church. Perhaps the following story will give an image to what we are saying.

THE *PORTIUNCOLA* OF ST. FRANCIS

Last summer my wife, Kris, and I vacationed in Italy. We visited Assisi, the home of St. Francis and St. Clare. Perched on top of a gentle Umbrian hill, Assisi peers out over a hazy, rich, and fertile plain. We Protestants have no "saints," but many of us claim Francis and Clare as our own. (Some of us see Francis as the first Protestant, and his story has been told well by Mark Galli in *Francis of Assisi and His World*.) We saw the historic places, including the Church of San Rufino, where the two saints were baptized, and the Basilica of St. Clare, where we stared with others at some of her relics. We participated in a worship service in the Basilica of St. Francis. We wandered with other tourists through the basilica to absorb as much as we could, paying special attention to the walls of the basilica, because they are "wallpapered" with Giotto's famous paintings depicting the Franciscan movement. It would take more knowledge of art and more time than we had to understand them all, but we tried.

Yes, I liked the basilica, but the most memorable part of the trip for me occurred after we left Assisi. We got into our rented Alfa Romeo and wound our way down from Assisi into the Umbrian plain to see two more churches. I had to see the *Portiuncola*. In the thirteenth century Francis restored this small church after it had crumbled to pieces, and it became the meeting point for the Franciscan friars. Famously small, the *Portiuncola* has become a stone parable of the humble life and ministry of Francis himself.

The *Portiuncola* was, of course, not large enough to house the crowds of pilgrims who would for centuries come to touch the Franciscan spirit. So St. Mary of the Angels was built to contain the crowds. We found St. Mary's easily enough, but we couldn't find the *Portiuncola*. I walked around the outside of the basilica but couldn't find St. Francis's little church. As we entered St. Mary's I asked a guide where the *Portiuncola* was, and he simply looked down into the basilica, pointed to a "church within a church," and said, "Right there."

There it was: Francis's original church, now completely restored, standing smack-dab in the middle of the basilica:

a church inside a church. I made a beeline through the basilica to the *Portiuncola*, entered into it, and just looked—trying to imagine my way into the world of Francis. Pilgrims were kneeling in prayer, while others were lost in meditation. By any account, the *Portiuncola* is a humble church of almost no distinction—except that St. Francis and the Franciscan movement owe part of their origins to this humble building.

The *Portiuncola* was humble. St. Mary of the Angels, as you might guess, was majestic and expansive and filled with all sorts of people, none of whom I knew but with whom I felt some kind of spiritual kinship. We had visited the *Portiuncola*, and we stood in the basilica with others, worshiping, praying, and drinking in the aesthetics of the place. I felt at home in both places—the *Portiuncola* and St. Mary of the Angels.

My intent for the Umbrian plain was to find the church of St. Francis, the *Portiuncola*, but what I discovered was that St. Francis's little church had been swallowed up by the movement that St. Francis created. I was seeking, as it were, Francis the individual, and what I discovered was a community that carried on his work. The gospel work of St. Francis spreads now across the globe, just as the work done on and in the *Portiuncola* was surrounded by St. Mary of the Angels.

The *Portiuncola* and the basilica. A church within a church. A little man inside a big movement. We need both. These are images for us to consider when it comes to understanding the two kinds of prayer.

PRAYER IS LIKE THAT

Prayer is both small and private and quiet and all alone (like the *Portiuncola*), and prayer is public and verbal and with others and in the open (like the basilica). Prayer is both private and public, both personal and communal. We may seek individual prayer, but the individual needs to be encompassed by the Church in prayer. We need both the personal and the communal—both are good; both are spiritually formative.

The theme of this book is this: As Christians, we are invited to pray both alone *in* the church (in our own *Portiuncola*) and together *with* the Church (in the basilica). We are invited to let our personal prayers be engulfed and enlarged by the prayers of the Church. We are invited to pray both *in* the church and *with* the Church.

Praying *with* the Church involves allowing our own prayer lives to be adjusted to the *sacred rhythms* of the Church's prayer tradition and invites us to use the words of the Bible and the Church. This book will focus on learning to pray *with* the Church, and it is an invitation for all Christians to learn to pray not just alone *in* the church but also together *with* the Church. There is nothing wrong with having our own *Portiuncola* kind of prayer—where we are alone with God, in our humble dwelling, and praying about our own concerns in a spontaneous fashion. I do this all the time.

But at times we are summoned out of our own prayer cells into the larger space where other Christians pray. I do this two or three times each day.

WHY SHOULD WE PRAY *WITH* THE CHURCH?

But why do we need this second form of prayer? The first answer is this: We pray in order to come into union with God. Prayer is talking to God, conversing with God, becoming intimate with God. By prayer we learn to love God. And the closer we come to God, the closer we come to God's people, for they surround God's heart.

The second answer to the question about why we need to pray *with* the Church is this: because we confess the *communion of saints*. This means we believe there is a spiritual unity among all Christians, all over the globe and all through history: Christians who are praying in heaven now and on earth below, saints who have gone before us and who will follow us. Sometimes we narrow our scope in this confession to those who are now alive with us, but the Church has always believed that we are ever surrounded by a "great cloud of witnesses" (as the author of the letter to the Hebrews puts it).

◆

Communion of the saints: "the fellowship which we enjoy with the saints and with those who have died in Christ." —PETER S. DAWES, THE NEW INTERNATIONAL DICTIONARY OF THE CHRISTIAN CHURCH

This communion of the saints revolves around a life of prayer and worship and service and love—for all times, world without end. Alleluia. Amen. So, the reason we need to get out of our own *Portiuncola* is that the Church is praying, too, and it asks us to join in the eternal chorus of praise and confession and worship and thanksgiving.

SO HOW DO WE PRAY *WITH* THE CHURCH?

We pray *with* the Church whenever we read or recite the Psalms, whenever we utter the Lord's Prayer (the Our Father) aloud, and whenever we learn to use the prayer books of the Church. That is, we pray *with* the Church when we pray at fixed times with the Church.

Quietly and unknown to many, there are Christians throughout the entire world—Protestants, Roman Catholics, Eastern Orthodox, and Christians of other stripes and hues—who gather together, open up the psalms or a prayer book, and "say their prayers" together. Many pray as an act of joining with the whole church, as an act that embodies the "communion of the saints," and as an act of solidarity in worship.

◆

Carol Showalter, author of 3D: Diet, Discipleship, and Discipline, *explained to me that she was in a gas station with a friend who was completely devoted to praying at fixed times. Carol's*

friend's little alarm went off, and the alarm was set to tell her friend this:
"Time to pray." She invited Carol to the corner of the gas station where
they had a short time of prayer. When it is time to pray, you pray,
wherever you might be.

In other words, we learn to pray *with* the Church when we practice the sacred rhythms of the day. Praying *with* the Church enables us to stand with Christians who are raising their hands at the same time in prayer. We are invited to join a revolving twenty-four-hour round of uninterrupted prayer offered by God's people all over the world.

THE UNITY OF PRAYING *WITH* THE CHURCH

We live in a fractured Church.

The Anglicans, or the Episcopalians in the USA, have a saying, *lex orandi, lex credendi*, meaning, "As we pray (or worship), so we believe." That is, though we may not agree in theology or even in Eucharistic practices, we can learn to pray and worship together.

◆

"In our community, we think of prayer as our common heartbeat, that
rhythmic and unceasing exchange of receiving and giving that sustains
our lives, both as a body and as individuals." —THE LITTLE BOOK
OF HOURS, X.

13

Praying together unites Christians. Jesus, after all, prayed for the unity of the Church when, as we are told in the seventeenth chapter of John's Gospel, he prayed that his followers might be one. *Lex orandi, lex credendi* is one way of working toward that goal of unity.

To do this we need to add prayer *with* the Church to our prayer *in* the church.

SUPPORTING ONE ANOTHER IN PRAYER

Prayer is difficult for many Christians. How many Christians pray even five minutes a day? There are lots of reasons for the lack of prayer: It takes time and effort. We are cramped in our schedules, and we are exhausted and gasping for some time to ourselves. Prayer requires concentration—serious concentration.

Sometimes we don't have the energy for prayer, and at other times we don't know what to say. If we are always in our own *Portiuncola* praying our own spontaneous prayers, we can eventually run out of things to say; our own spontaneous prayers can become, ironically, vain repetitions themselves. But learning to pray set prayers at fixed times according to a sacred rhythm can reinvigorate our prayer lives and lift the burden of creativity off our shoulders.

MY OWN STORY

Whether we pray in our own *Portiuncola* or in a basilica, prayer takes time, and it requires commitment. I have struggled with prayer my entire Christian life. Apart from a couple of seasons of my life when prayer seemed to be both natural and effective, I have struggled most of my adult life when it comes to regular prayer. Not that I don't pray: I've always prayed for my family, especially for Kris and our two children. And I've prayed about my day and expressed my concerns to God in the quiet of my study or in the midst of the day's activities. I've routinely dedicated my work for the day to God's glory. But prayer has been a struggle.

I now understand that the heart of my struggle was that I knew only one form of prayer: spontaneous prayer in my own *Portiuncola*. I grew tired of carrying the same little basket of prayers to God every day. But comments by friends a few years back prompted me to look again at prayer in the Bible and in the Church, and to take a fresh look at the prayer-book tradition of the Church.

As I studied, I began to see how God made Israel's life rhythmical: He gave them a calendar full of holy days. He directed them to come often to spend a day at the tabernacle or the temple, where worship and sacrifice were set into sacred rhythm. Israel's history reveals a continuous rhythm of sacred, communal prayer.

When I (re)discovered that Jesus lived according to those rhythms, I began to see them in the early Christian churches. It was then that I saw how significant prayer books were for the history of the Church. And only then did I say, "It's time for me to experience sacred prayer rhythms." This book is the result of that journey, a journey of struggling in my own *Portiuncola* and finding that the prayers of others have given me new words to say, new praises to utter, and new friends to support me.

This journey led me to see that there are two kinds of prayer in the Bible: spontaneous individual prayers and communal prayers. The first kind of prayer, praying *in* the church, can be seen in the life of Brother Lawrence, who learned to pray constantly by learning to dwell in the presence of God. The widely read book *The Practice of the Presence of God* describes how he lived in God's presence and in constant communion with God. This type of prayer was a good fit with the tradition I grew up in.

◆

I have left off all devotions and prayers which are not required for me, and I occupy myself solely with keeping myself in God's holy presence. I do this simply by keeping my attention on God and by being generally and lovingly aware of Him. This could be called practicing the presence of God moment by moment, or to put it better, a silent, secret and nearly unbroken conversation of the soul with God.

—BROTHER LAWRENCE

But my journey led me to discover the second kind of prayer, praying *with* the Church. This kind of prayer is usually associated with prayer books. My first experience with a prayer book was with the Anglican *Book of Common Prayer*, the most widely used Protestant prayer book. My wife's maternal grandmother's copy of the *BCP* sat on one of my bookshelves for years: Leather-bound, gilt edges. Onion-skin paper. Very nice looking. Occasionally I would pull it down and look through it—but not having been taught to use it, I found it confusing.

As I continued my study, however, I saw that prayer books are used in many traditions of the Church, and that they provide a means for Christians to live according to sacred rhythms just as Jesus himself did. My instinctive fear of repetition gave way to an understanding that sometimes I just didn't have the words to say what was on my heart, but the "old, old" words of prayer books could express my thoughts better than I could by myself.

My journey showed me that I was following in the footsteps of millions of God's people who have gone before me. "Come along," Jesus, the Bible, and the Church say, "and you'll discover what many are discovering today: Praying *with* the Church can re-shape the soul."

MY OWN PRACTICE

So many people are interested in using prayer books that some new ones have appeared. These can, as it were, open the door from your own *Portiuncola* into the wider basilica.

A few years back I began using Phyllis Tickle's modern prayer book, *The Divine Hours*. Whenever Kris and I are together in the morning or evening, we pull out *The Divine Hours* and read from it aloud and we "say our prayers." When I am traveling, I carry a copy with me, and I pray *with* the Church—sometimes in airports or hotels. On days I teach, I get to my office, turn on the lights, start my computer, and then sit down in a comfortable chair in my office and read the morning prayers for that day before heading to class.

And I always do this aloud, or at least at a mumble level, making sure I am doing more than just glancing at the psalms or prayers. Glancing at prayers is the fastest path toward vain repetitions I know of. For that reason, the church has always advocated reading our prayers aloud so we will go more slowly and concentrate more on what we are saying. Prayer books are designed to be read aloud.

I use *The Divine Hours*, but I also change prayer books. Sometimes I use *A Manual of Eastern Orthodox Prayers*, and sometimes I use *The Liturgy of the Hours*. Sometimes I use *Benedictine Daily Prayer*, and sometimes I use *The Book of Common Prayer*. Sometimes I use *The Glenstal Book of Prayer* or *The Little Book of Hours: Praying with the Community of Jesus*. Sometimes I use other books. You no doubt may find yet others. In my own practice, I establish variety as a rule. Each prayer book invites me to pray with the Church with set prayers at fixed hours.

This book is designed to help you learn how to use the great prayer books of the Church. It is not designed to eliminate spontaneous prayers but to complement that kind of prayer with the inclusive, beautiful prayers that the Church has prayed for centuries.

If you want to pray better, I can think of no better way than to learn to pray *with* the Church by using its prayer books. Certainly, we need to pray whatever is on our heart, when we want to—that is spontaneous prayer. But, the Church has also prayed together, and this book encourages us to learn to pray also with the church.

◆

A new study about the prayer life of pastors, who are our supposed to be our leaders in prayer, shows that about half of them are dissatisfied with their prayer lives. In fact, only nine percent of younger pastors are satisfied with their times of prayer. Many dissatisfied pastors are discovering that a life of prayer is stimulated by the use of prayer books.

COME, JOIN ALONG

In this book I'm inviting you to leave your own *Portiuncola* two or three times a day to join the saints of God in the church—so we can learn to pray together, not only alone *in* the church, but also together *with* the Church.

PART ONE

JESUS AND DAILY RHYTHMS OF PRAYER

2

PRAYING WITH JESUS:
SACRED TIME, SACRED TERM

'm a low-church Protestant, and a stubborn one at that. That means that the Bible is the foundation of what I believe and what I do. If I can be shown that something is in the Bible, I'm all for it—except for things like greeting one another with a holy kiss or washing one another's feet. If some idea or practice is not from the Bible or at least from the practice of Jesus and the early Christians, then I'm less sanguine about believing it or doing it. This is how many of us Protestants practice what is called *sola scriptura*, the Reformation principle of "Scripture alone." Actually, what I've just stated is a simplistic understanding even of the principle, but it will work for this context. Many of us want to know that what we believe and do is from the Bible.

When it comes to praying, I want to know what the Bible says. How does Jesus want me to pray? How did Jesus himself pray? What did Jesus teach about prayer? As a Protestant, this is where I begin. What the Church taught, is teaching, and will teach is secondary for me to what the Bible and, in particular, Jesus, says.

For all of us, beginning with Jesus himself and continuing to each of us today, prayer is talking to God, either alone or with others. Humans opening their hearts to God, saying what is on their minds, telling God the utter truth about themselves and what they are feeling—that's what prayer is. But each of us understands "talking to God" in our own particular way.

Each of us makes our way in life with a "prayer tradition"— the one that comes packaged with our family and our denomination and our friends. This tradition teaches us what to pray, how to pray, and when to pray. This way of praying seems quite natural and simple until someone joins us from another path and suggests a different way of praying.

While I was still in college, I remember going merrily along in the way of my own prayer tradition when a fellow Christian suggested that I learn to pray in tongues— which was the prayer tradition he was familiar with. Not only had I never heard someone pray in tongues, I hadn't even imagined doing such a thing myself. We've all been joined in our journey by those who come from a different prayer tradition, and listening to their journey can help us on ours.

Here's the question we need to ask more often: What if Jesus joined us? What would he say about how we are to pray? Would he pray only in his own *Portiuncola* or would he also pray out in the expansive basilica and ask us to join him? What prayer practices would he suggest? What ideas about prayer would he have for us to think about?

I've spent thirty years of my life studying about Jesus and reading books by those who also study about Jesus, and I've discovered that Jesus focused on four elements of prayer, four simple points, two of which will be covered in the rest of this chapter.

Sacred time: learning when to pray

Sacred term: learning what to call God

Sacred rhythms: learning what time of day to pray

Sacred prayers: learning what to say

SACRED TIME:
LEARNING WHEN TO PRAY

Jesus prayed all the time. The opening chapter of the Gospel of Mark tells us that "In the morning, while it was still very dark, [Jesus] got up and went out to a deserted place, and there he prayed." The disciples searched Jesus out and found him: The implication is that the disciples knew where Jesus was and what he was most likely doing. In other words, praying early in the morning (in his own *Portiuncola*) was Jesus' habit.

◆

The Psalms [the prayer book Jesus used] . . . confirm that we can know God's presence at all times only if we set aside certain times for prayer. The Jews did not buy into a more current notion that since God is present everywhere and in all times we can pray whenever we feel like it. Rather, they believed that praying regularly at set and specific times helps focus and reorient one to God at all other times.

—ARTHUR PAUL BOERS

If *Praying with the Church* focuses on learning to pray *with* the Church, it does not intend to overlook the importance of personal, spontaneous prayers. Anyone who desires to follow Jesus' own example and teachings will find harmony between praying alone *in* the church and praying together *with* the Church. So, it is good for us to begin with this element in Jesus' life: He prayed alone. Constantly.

Jesus often withdrew quietly into his own *Portiuncola* to pray. When his fame as a healer grew rapidly, the fifth chapter of the Gospel of Luke tells us that Jesus' response was to "withdraw to deserted places and pray." In the next chapter, Luke tells us that Jesus "went out to the mountain to pray; and he spent the night in prayer to God."

Jesus discerned when big moments in his life were about to occur, and he plunged himself into prayer to face them. In the third chapter of the Gospel of Luke, the Gospel that emphasizes Jesus' prayer life, Luke says Jesus was praying at his *baptism*: "Now when all the people were baptized, and when Jesus also had been baptized and was praying, the heaven was opened." Again, before the *selection of the twelve*, he prayed as noted in the sixth chapter of Luke's Gospel: "Now during those days he went out to the mountain to pray; and he spent the night in prayer to God. And when day came, he called his disciples and chose twelve of them, whom he also named apostles." Jesus prayed all the time, and therefore following his example is to learn to join him on the path by constantly turning our heart toward God.

One who learned to pray always (as Jesus did) was G. K. Chesterton, who developed what can only be called a happy countenance about a life that brought him endless delights. He became a person who prayed all the time:

You say grace before meals
All right.
But I say grace before the play and the opera,
And grace before the concert and pantomime,
And grace before I open a book,
And grace before sketching, painting,
Swimming, fencing, foxing, walking, playing, dancing;
And grace before I dip the pen in ink.

Since Chesterton was a prolific writer, if he said grace each time before he dipped his pen in ink, he must have prayed all the time.

There is a long-standing Christian tradition of "praying constantly." It derives from the fifth chapter of Paul's letter to the Thessalonians, and a standard translation is this: "Pray without ceasing." At one level, this is impossible—how can I be constantly praying and, at the same time, concentrate on driving in rush-hour traffic? In the history of the church, there have been two interpretations: Either Paul is exhorting us to be in a constant attitude of prayerfulness or (as I tend to think) we are to devote ourselves to the sacred rhythms of prayer. There is plenty of biblical support for either view, and one can appeal to Jesus' example for both. Perhaps we should say "we don't know" and opt for both viewpoints.

◆

We started to follow the morning office a little over one year ago. We have been following the Celtic Daily Prayer *from the Northumbria Community. There are five of us who day in and day out show up at the church at 7:00 AM, rain or shine (or, like today, snow). I wasn't sure how it was going to go over, or how long it would last, but it just keeps on going. The days we don't feel like coming in, God tends to show up and we all leave feeling refreshed.*

We did the complete office during a 24/7 prayer session this summer (morning, noon, vespers, & compline). That was hard, but there was something special, especially during the night offices. I don't know what it is, but it feels like we are doing something bigger than us, something that cuts through time. —JOE HOLDA

SACRED TERM:
LEARNING WHAT TO CALL GOD

Jesus not only prayed all the time, he also began his prayer on a distinct note—a note that itself tells the story of Jesus' own prayer life. Jesus almost always began his prayers with *Abba*, the Aramaic word for "Father." Some have overstretched this term to suggest that Jesus was the first person in Jewish history to call God *Abba*, or the first Jew to be truly intimate with God. Still, Jesus' emphasis on God as *Abba* is distinct—*Abba* was his favorite term for God; he began his prayers with that word, and he taught his followers to begin their prayers by calling God *Abba*.

That is the sacred name of God for Jesus: Call God "Abba," he taught his followers.

For Jesus, though, calling God *Abba* was more than a theological statement. As the English scholar G. B. Caird has put it so well: "For Jesus the Fatherhood of God had become a profoundly religious experience, long before it became a doctrine to be communicated to others." That is, Jesus' calling God *Abba* is a window into the heart of his religious experience, into the relationship Jesus had with his Father. In this sense, the term *Abba* tells the whole story of Jesus' own prayer life and what he teaches his followers: God is (as John Ortberg says) "closer than you think" and is more available than you think and is more intimate than you think. Prayer for Jesus is about calling God *Abba*.

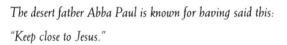

The desert father Abba Paul is known for having said this:
"Keep close to Jesus."

The lessons Jesus gave his followers on prayer are many, but they are learned mostly by praying and not by reading a textbook about prayer. Jesus taught them to pray honestly, to pray simply, to pray persistently, to pray humbly, to center their constant thoughts on God, and to pray together. Jesus prayed before he ate, and he gave thanks for good things. He told parables about prayer.

But it was Jesus' own example—of praying all the time and of calling God *Abba*—that struck his disciples and should strike us today. If we are to learn from Jesus, we will do well to begin with this: We need to open our hearts to God on a constant basis with the trust that God wants us to share our lives with him so he can share his life with us.

As we imagine what it would be like for Jesus to teach us in the way of prayer, we are suggesting that Jesus would teach us to pray all the time and to call God *Abba,* following the example of how he entered his very own *Portiuncola* for a life of constant, personal prayer. But there is more to Jesus' own prayer life than praying alone—for Jesus was one in whom the ancient Israelite prayer traditions came alive.

3

PRAYING WITH JESUS:
SACRED RHYTHMS

*J*esus prayed within the sacred rhythms of Israel, and he knew firsthand their formative influence. So, if he joined us on our journey, we'd soon discover that two or three times a day he'd ask us to leave our own *Portiuncola* to venture into the basilica as he turned his body and his heart, with millions of others, toward God to say some rather familiar, sacred rhythmical prayers.

◆

Fixed-hour prayer, praying the psalms and the Lord's Prayer, serve to kind of "stitch" my day with time spent consciously worshiping God. Regardless of where I've been or what I'm involved in, knowing I can come back to the place of prayer and worship draws me deeper into God. —STACEY LITTLEFIELD

When it dawned on me—and the light had to work through some crusty layers of prejudice and history—that Jesus participated in the prayer life of his people, such as praying the Psalms, repeating the Lord's Prayer, and reciting the revered *Shema* ("Hear, O Israel!") twice a day, I shifted my own beliefs and prayer practices and began to pray both alone *in* the church and together *with* the Church. Not only did I pray in my *Portiuncola*, but also I left it a few times a day, walked into the wide expanse of the basilica, and joined millions of Christians praying at fixed hours. I changed because of what I understood Jesus and the Bible taught, and because of what I have learned about both how Israel prayed and how the early Christians prayed.

Pausing for the "hours" of prayer during the day transcends personal prayer time in our own *Portiuncola*. Perhaps this needs to be emphasized here: The commitment to pause with Jesus so we can pray *with* the Church is a conscious decision on our part to join other Christians and to pray with them as part of our devotion to the Lord. Praying *with* the Church, then, is more than praying personally according to the sacred rhythms of the hours of prayer.

SACRED RHYTHMS FROM THE BIBLE

We don't know a great deal about the prayer life of ancient Israel, but we do know that it was customary for pious Jews to interrupt the day to pray at three separate times. The word "interrupt" is too harsh; it would be better to say that the Jewish day was punctuated or ordered by three sacred prayer rhythms. It would have been nearly impossible for Jesus to have been a Jew in the first century, at least a pious Jew, and not to have participated in Israel's sacred prayer rhythm of praying *with* the community of faith.

Jesus' custom of praying three times a day with others didn't appear out of nowhere. It is found in the Bible—if you are willing to listen, as I wasn't for so many years. Several examples show us when people of faith prayed. Psalm 55 says this (with my added italics):

But I call upon God,
    and the LORD will save me.
Evening and *morning* and at *noon*
      I utter my complaint and moan,
      and he will hear my voice.

Three times a day—evening, morning, and noon, the psalmist says—he complains to God, and he is confident God is listening. The psalmist begins with "evening" because the Jewish day begins at sundown. (Some modern translations convert this Jewish ordering of the day into a more modern one and read "morning, noon, and evening.")

The great prophet Daniel was known for praying sacred rhythmical prayers three times a day, even though he knew praying in public could cost him his life! In chapter six of his prophecies we read this:

Although Daniel knew that the document [to arrest and imprison in a lions' den anyone who prayed to anyone other than the Persian King Darius] had been signed, he continued to go to his house, which had windows in its upper room open toward Jerusalem, and to get down on his knees three times a day to pray to his God and praise him, just as he had done previously.

At the time of Daniel, and perhaps as early as the time of the psalmists, Jews were committed to fixed hours of prayer. When? When they got up, in the middle of the day, and when they went to bed. Morning, afternoon, and evening.

Here we have two examples of ancient Israelites pausing during the day to pray, and time has shown us that what they were doing was joining others who were doing the same thing at the same time.

Jesus refers to this fixed rhythm of prayer when he criticizes the hypocrites for the delightful happenstance of finding themselves conveniently in a public forum at the time of afternoon prayer so they could, ironically, pray *with* others so they would be seen *by* the others. Notice this from Matthew 6:

And whenever you pray, do not be like the hypocrites; for they love to stand and pray in the synagogues and at the street corners, so that they may be seen by others [during early evening prayers].

Jesus does not criticize the hypocrites for praying *with* other Israelites but for praying with other Israelites *in order to be noticed* by them.

That the early Christians participated in this sacred rhythm of three-times-a-day prayer can be seen in the example of the apostles Peter and John, as recorded in the third chapter of Acts:

34

One day Peter and John were going up to the temple at the hour of prayer, at three o'clock in the afternoon.

These two apostles were accustomed to attending temple prayers "at the hour of prayer, at three o'clock in the afternoon." The original Greek says they did this at the "ninth hour," that is, the ninth hour from sunup, which would be about three in the afternoon. What the apostles did when they got to the temple was pray *with* the community of faith that gathered at the time of the afternoon sacrifice to join the temple leaders in prayer for Israel.

Outside the New Testament, a document called the *Didache*, an early manual on the Christian life from around the turn of the first century, tells us that the Christians prayed the Lord's Prayer three times a day. The text doesn't tell us what the times were, but history suggests it was morning, afternoon, and evening prayers that included the Lord's Prayer.

From David to Daniel, from the Jewish world to the Christian world, the sacred rhythm of prayer was a three-times-a-day routine of praying *with* the community of faith. This was the world of the Jews, this was the world of Jesus, and this was the world of the early Christians.

We need to advance one step now: What is important for us today for spiritual formation is that time for Jesus was shaped by a three-times-a-day sacred rhythm. Time was measured by the hours of prayer.

◆

A story about St. Macrina (d. 370), the sister of the great theologian Gregory of Nyssa: On the last night of her life, when the local community of faith gathered to hear more of her wisdom, her brother writes: While she was saying this, I kept wishing that the day could be lengthened so that she might not cease to delight our hearing; but the singing of the choir was calling us to evening thanksgiving prayers, and the great Macrina sent me off to church too and withdrew herself [she was a nun] to God in prayer. And the night was spent in these devotions.

But you and I today, in the twenty-first century, fall into the idea that time is something measured by a clock—when we get to work and when we end work, when we get up and when we go to bed. Or perhaps we measure time by when we eat—breakfast and lunch and dinner. We can too easily become "time-clock humans" or even "meal-driven people" by how our time is regulated. Is there another way? There is: That other way is to let the hours of prayer shape our days. The blessings of life that enter most deeply into our soul do not come by our finding more free time or more leisure. Those blessings enter the soul when we let soul rhythms, the sacred rhythms of prayer, shape the structure of our day.

◆

For the last several years my spiritual life has been greatly impacted through praying the "Jesus Prayer"* and through the use of an Orthodox prayer rope. I was inspired to attempt this after reading Nouwen's Reaching Out *and the anonymous* The Way of the Pilgrim. *Although the Jesus Prayer is one of the simplest prayers, its transformative power has been profound. Coming from a decidedly non-liturgical background, I have begun to find great benefit not only in the Jesus Prayer but in* The Book of Common Prayer *as well.*

—Paul Hill

Jews at the time of Jesus measured time in a variety of ways—none of them by a clock. There were morning prayers and late afternoon prayers and evening prayers, each of which was tied somehow to the worship of the temple. Time was not rooted simply in the economic system or in meal routines but more fundamentally by the temple's worship. Imagine a clock that did not say "3 PM" but "afternoon sacrifice."

Jesus came of age in a Judaism shaped by a three-times-a-day-we-all-stop-and-pray-together sacred rhythm. This sacred sense of time shaped Jesus, and it shaped how the early followers of Jesus learned to pray with Jesus and with the church. The so-called "hours" of prayer were not one- or two-hour-long prayer marathons that wandered the

---

* The Jesus Prayer, "Lord Jesus Christ, have mercy on me, a sinner," is discussed in chapter seven, below.

37

globe in prayer requests while little children groaned the question, "How long before we are done?" Nor were they times when Jewish males opened their scrolls of Torah, pulled out some Bible-study reference tools, and went to work on a passage of Scripture. No, these sacred hours of prayer were a designated "hour" (such as 3 PM) set aside from the day for several minutes to recite together Israel's richest treasures of prayer. Nor were they times when the pious had a quiet time as they contemplated their own spiritual growth.

The hours of prayer created another sense of spiritual formation, that we are formed together as we learn to pray together. These ancient Jews and Christians uttered sacred prayers together. They did this every day—together. These prayers established sacred rhythms to their days and lives as a community.

And they can do the same today. For us. As the Church. As a community of faith.

REDISCOVERING THE SACRED HOURS OF PRAYER FOR TODAY

Spiritual formation for Jews at the time of Jesus was shaped by this sacred prayer rhythm. It can do the same for us, and the testimonials that can be read in these chapters illustrate precisely that: The discovery of the "hours" of prayer is the discovery of ancient wisdom for how the people of God daily direct themselves toward God in praise and worship and petition.

◆

Technical civilization is man's conquest of space. It is a triumph frequently achieved by sacrificing an essential ingredient of existence, namely, time. . . . But time is the heart of existence. . . . We can only master time in time. . . . We must not forget that it is not a thing that lends significance to a moment; it is the moment that lends significance to things. —ABRAHAM JOSHUA HESCHEL

But, the development of sacred rhythms for praying has never been about establishing exact rules and times. For some, of course, this is a part of their faith commitment. If we join a community that follows the "hours" of prayer, there will undoubtedly be specified times for prayer. But for the rest of us, sacred prayer rhythms are not required of us but are provided as a way for us to hallow each portion of each day—morning, afternoon, and evening—a way of offering that portion of the day to God, of keeping our lives centered on the invitation from God to love God with all of our heart, soul, mind, and strength. In other words, living within the sweet caresses of the hours of prayer is the simplest and easiest way to consecrate our entire day as service to God. At the same time it is the simplest way to express what we all believe in: the communion of the saints in prayer and worship.

Rhythmical prayer sounds simple: Just stop what you are doing a few times in the day to pray with others, whether we see these others or not. But, there are very few things in life as hard as establishing good habits. Countless Christians can tell you of the New Year's resolutions they make to pray regularly or to read their Bibles daily or to attend church services weekly. Many of those Christians can also tell you that by January 10 they have failed and given up on that resolution for that year. Why? It is hard for us to change. It is hard to begin a new habit or to establish a new rhythm in life.

Establishing a personal sacred rhythm of praying with the Church is a challenge. But, what many people find the most helpful for establishing rhythmical prayer is to connect a prayer time with a natural break in the day—before one sits down to eat breakfast, after one has eaten dinner, before one falls asleep, at the time our employers schedule a break. Others, as in the example mentioned above, use the alarm clock and have the will to stop whatever they are doing to pause to pray. Some learn to pause for prayer when the church bells ring. Others keep a prayer book and a Bible next to their bed and spend time with them when they rise or before they fall asleep or both. Apart from the structure created by church bells at the hours of prayer, most find the opportunity for creating a sacred rhythm by associating it with a schedule shift in the day—between showering and breakfast, between breakfast and reading the paper, during the commute to work, at morning break, just before or after lunch, at the afternoon break, before or after dinner, or at bedtime.

The wisdom is simple: Find a break that works for you and then stick to it until it becomes a habit.

◆

I was "nannying" last summer and discovered a sacred rhythm that worked for me: During my commute, I would come to a slow four-way stop; when I got there, I paused and said the "Jesus Creed" [a version of the Shema and Jesus' own teachings], and that moment of time with the Lord gave me perspective and strength for the day.

—RENEE DINGES

I find the rhythm of praying with the Church in the morning and evening easier to do, but I find it nearly impossible to pause during the middle of a busy workday to slow down to say prayers. This has always been hard, I suspect, especially for those of us who find our work to be a delight—and I think work is itself a form of prayer. I am writing this at 1:15 PM on a day when I did not pause for midday prayers, yet I am writing a book on the value of pausing for midday prayers!

What I am suggesting about Jewish prayer at the time of Jesus, and about Jesus' own sacred rhythms, is that a sacred rhythm of praying with others is both a calling and a challenge. We should do what we can. There is no reason to turn what should be a delightful time of prayer into an iron-heavy burden we are to carry about during our days. We are, after all, in good company, since we are doing what Jesus and his disciples and countless saints have done before us, and what countless numbers of Christians are doing *with* us.

◆

I started [praying] with Phyllis Tickle's The Divine Hours *about a year ago, though I can't remember what got my attention initially. At any rate, I value the approach for a number of reasons: (1) It removes the emotional component. Whether or not I "feel" like it, this is what I do. I pray and worship. (2) It connects me to the church across time. Some of these prayers have been recited for centuries. Vespers [evening prayer] today included a hymn written before Columbus sailed to America. (3) Similarly, it connects me to the church across space. These prayers are being said around the globe. (4) The recurring nature keeps me connected, balanced like I'm coming back to a touchstone periodically. It is a way to abide or dwell in Christ. It provides a baseline of worship and prayer for daily life.*

—Cory Aldrich

4

PRAYING WITH JESUS:
SACRED PRAYERS

We have seen that Jesus taught that all of time was sacred time, that his followers were to address God with a sacred term ("Abba"), and that daily life was to be structured by sacred rhythms. We now need to see that Jesus taught some sacred prayers that his followers were to recite and use as the foundation for life.

If you and I are to leave our own *Portiuncola* two or three times a day to pray *with* the Church in the wide-open basilica filled with Christians all over the world, it is natural for us to ask these questions: "What will we be saying? Did Jesus teach anything about that? Won't it get repetitive to say things over and over?" Our answers echo the history of God's people: "We'll be using the prayers of the Bible, of Jesus, and the Church. Yes, it will be repetitive but in a good way. Praying *with* the Church might lead to vain repetitions, but it is meant to lead us *away* from them."

Once again, the wise tradition of rhythmical prayer in the Bible offers guidance. We are now ready to listen to Jesus' fourth lesson about prayer, but before we do that, let's remind ourselves of the Jewish form of prayer in use at the time of Jesus.

WHAT DID THE JEWS SAY AT FIXED HOURS OF PRAYER?

Jews prayed at fixed hours—morning, afternoon, and evening. This was the sacred rhythm of the temple and of Israel at prayer together. But what did they say?

◆

"These three hours of prayer, together with the benedictions said before and after meals, were Israel's great treasure, the skeleton framework for an education in prayer and for the practice of prayer for everyone from their youth upwards."

—JOACHIM JEREMIAS, NEW TESTAMENT SCHOLAR

Above all, Jews routinely recited the Psalms when they prayed. Look again at the book of Psalms, and you will observe that it is a collection of 150 prayers bundled together. The reason we have this bundle of prayers is that it was used by Israel for corporate and private prayer. The book of Psalms is not a collection of (only) David's prayers because David wanted to see his prayers in print. No, the book of Psalms is a collection of prayers deemed useful for and by all of Israel. These psalms were chanted aloud in the temple and the synagogue, and Israelites learned to join along by memorizing them.

Everything Israel and Jesus learned about prayer can be found in the Psalms.

In addition to praying using the Psalms (sometimes the book of Psalms is called "the Psalter"), Jews recited set prayers and creeds. The day began in Israel at sundown, so the prayer routines begin at that time. A pious Jew began the sacred rhythm of prayers by reciting the *Shema*: "Hear, O Israel! The Lord our God, the Lord is One. Love the Lord your God with all your heart, with all your soul, and with all your strength." Moses, in the sixth chapter of Deuteronomy, commands Israel to recite this *Shema* in the evening and the morning. Here are the words of Moses (in italics) that explain how the *Shema* was to be practiced:

Memorize them: *Keep these words that I am commanding you today in your heart.*

Teach them: *Recite them to your children and talk about them when you are at home and when you are away, when you lie down and when you rise* [evening and morning].

Make it physical: *Bind them as a sign on your hand, fix them as an emblem on your forehead.*

Publish them: *[W]rite them on the doorposts of your house and on your gates.*

From what we know, most Jews practiced this: Every evening and morning began with the *Shema*. The Jewish historian Josephus puts it this way in the fourth chapter of his *Jewish Antiquities*: "Twice a day, at its beginning and when the hour of sleep approaches, it is fitting to remember in gratitude before God the gifts which he gave us after the deliverance from Egypt." The primary gift Josephus was thinking of was the

Torah, perfectly summed up as it was in the *Shema*. Reciting the *Shema* defined who was and who wasn't obedient. Rabbi Eliezer ben Hyrcanus, at the end of the first century, said it like this: "Who is an *Am ha-aretz*? [Who disregards the Law?] He who does not recite the *Shema* in the morning and in the evening."

The Christian practice of morning and evening prayer derives from this singular commandment for Israel. The *Shema* wove itself so tightly around the faith of ancient Israel that it would have been impossible for followers of Jesus not to adopt (and adapt) the custom of turning to God at sundown and sunup.

An unquestionable practice of Jews at the time of Jesus was the daily recitation of the *Shema*. Jews probably also recited the Ten Commandments. The Nash Papyrus, which appears to have been made more than a century earlier than the birth of Jesus, is a single sheet of papyrus that joins the Ten Commandments with the *Shema*. Many today think the Nash Papyrus indicates that the Ten Commandments were recited together with the *Shema*. This suggestion is slightly confirmed by observing that, when Jesus addressed the rich young ruler, Jesus combined a listing of some of the Ten Commandments with Jesus' own version of the *Shema*, which I call "the Jesus Creed." Thus, Jesus says to the rich young ruler: "You shall not murder; You shall not commit adultery; You shall not steal; You shall not bear false witness; Honor your father and mother." Then, he added, "You shall love your neighbor as yourself." Here we find a combination of some of the Ten Commandments with the second half of the

Jesus Creed. This is possible evidence that Jews recited the Ten Commandments together with the *Shema*.

◆

THE SHEMA
Deuteronomy 6:4-5

Hear, O Israel: The LORD is our God, the LORD alone. You shall love the LORD your God with all your heart, and with all your soul, and with all your might.

THE TEN COMMANDMENTS
Exodus 20:2–17 (abbr.)

I am the LORD your God, who brought you out of the land of Egypt, out of the house of slavery.

#1: *You shall have no other gods before me.*

#2: *You shall not make for yourself an idol, whether in the form of anything that is in heaven above, or that is on the earth beneath, or that is in the water under the earth.*

#3: *You shall not make wrongful use of the name of the LORD your God, for the LORD will not acquit anyone who misuses his name.*

#4: *Remember the Sabbath day, and keep it holy.*

#5: *Honor your father and your mother, so that your days may be long in the land that the LORD your God is giving you.*

#6: *You shall not murder.*

#7: *You shall not commit adultery.*

#8: *You shall not steal.*

#9:You shall not bear false witness against your neighbor.

#10:You shall not covet your neighbor's house; you shall not covet your neighbor's wife, or male or female slave, or ox, or donkey, or anything that belongs to your neighbor.

In addition to the *Shema* (and perhaps the Ten Commandments), Jews at the time of Jesus also prayed a prayer known by three names: the *Amidah* ("standing prayer"), the *Shemoneh Esreh* (Eighteen Benedictions), or the *Ha-Tefillah* ("The Prayer"). Because moderns call it the *Amidah*, I will use that term for this customary daily prayer. Several petitions of this prayer follow:

Blessed art thou, Lord, God of our fathers, God of Abraham, God of Isaac and God of Jacob, great, mighty and fearful God, most high God who createst heaven and earth, our shield and the shield of our fathers, our trust in every generation.
Blessed art thou, Lord, shield of Abraham.

Grant us, our Father, the knowledge (that comes) from thee, and understanding and discernment (that come) from thy Torah.
Blessed art thou, Lord, who grantest knowledge.

Bring thy peace over Israel, thy people, and over thy city and over thine inheritance; and bless all of us together.
Blessed art thou, Lord, who makest peace.

48

These three set confessions and prayers, the *Shema*, perhaps the Ten Commandments, and the *Amidah*, are what Jews said at the time of Jesus when they participated in the sacred rhythms of praying with Israel at the hours of prayer. They no doubt prayed other things—spontaneous things— but those times were shaped by the *Shema*, perhaps the Ten Commandments, and the *Amidah*.

The reason these three set forms were used is obvious: They express the central dimensions of Israel's faith and concerns with clarity and aesthetic simplicity. Any person who recites these elements and reflects upon them will have some of the central features of Israel's faith pulsed into the chambers of the heart. That heart would beat to the rhythms of loving God, obeying central commandments for the good of others, and praying for what most glorifies God. The secret to a soul formation created by sacred rhythms emerges from focusing on what is most central to the faith and letting it seep into the inner workings of our hearts by reciting it often enough to keep it in front of us.

A JEWISH PRAYER DAY

Here, then, is what a Jewish day of prayer would have looked like— in addition to the ongoing spontaneous prayers that they would have been praying and the use of the Psalter that permeated both these hours of prayer and their spontaneous prayers.

MORNING	AFTERNOON	EVENING
Shema		*Shema*
(*10 Commandments*)		(*10 Commandments*)
Amidah	*Amidah*	*Amidah*

SACRED RHYTHMS, SACRED PRAYERS

Those of us who grew up in the *Portiuncola* and who have never participated in liturgical prayers in the basilica, and who are innately suspicious of repeated prayers may say, "But, surely, the recitation of something ancient leads to vain repetitions."

◆

For the most part, I have found myself blessed in ways I wouldn't have imagined [by praying set prayers]. First, prayer now controls me more than I control prayer. My "self" is forced to subjugate itself to something that is greater and far more holy then I. Second, using a lectionary takes me into Scriptures that I normally wouldn't visit, [and this] usually opens up some surprising vistas. Third, reading and praying according to a set schedule gives a rhythm to life that is sadly lacking in our modern world. This brings about a centeredness, a sense of being grounded, a home to come back to again and again for refreshment, forgiveness, and encouragement. My devotional and spiritual life is much richer for following the prayer guides. —DAN WHITMARSH*

Yes, it can, but it need not. Repetition, like saying "I love you" to someone dear to us, can become a rhythm for daily renewal just as easily as it can become a mindless routine.

But let's probe this concern about repetition in another way. This question may actually be masking another issue, one that is part of the hesitation to use prayers written by others. Our tendency is to go to the Bible for something new, to read it in the expectation of a fresh discovery of something we did not know or had not heard or had completely forgotten. As a professor who teaches the Bible, I know the experience.

But the discovery of something new is not the sole, or even the main, purpose for reading the Bible. The longer you look at the idea that we read the Bible to find new meanings, the sillier it becomes. We read and return to the Bible not (just) to find something new but to hear something old, not to discover something fresh but to be reminded of something ancient.

What we find in the sacred rhythm and sacred prayer tradition of Israel is the wise recitation of those passages in the Bible most central to spirituality, passages we need to be reminded of daily because of their importance for how we are to conduct ourselves before God and with others. The reason psalms are repeated in the sacred rhythm of prayer is that they continue to teach us how to pray; the reason the *Shema* is repeated so often is that it summons us to the central orientation of our heart: to love God with every molecule we can muster.

◆

[T]his Presbyterian has been using fixed prayers (the daily office) for years, and I find it indispensable. My thoughts are too jumbled, my mind too wandering, without some [set prayer] form.

—CRAIG HIGGINS

Jesus was spiritually nurtured by pious parents in a world where the sacred rhythm of prayer shaped spiritual formation. Jesus didn't adopt that rhythm without reflection or alteration. One might say that Jesus actually re-shaped the sacred rhythmical prayer practices of his world so that they would reflect his own kingdom mission.

5

PRAYING WITH JESUS:
SACRED TRADITION

*J*esus as a pious Jew prayed both spontaneously and with others. In pausing throughout the day, he reminded himself daily of the importance of loving God by reciting the *Shema*, perhaps the Ten Commandments, and probably the *Amidah*. Now we can ask, "What did Jesus say when he prayed? Did he offer any alternatives to the *Amidah*? Did he make any contributions to the sacred rhythmical prayer tradition of Israel?"

Jesus established the foundation for a new tradition of sacred rhythmical prayer. There are three elements to Jesus' sacred tradition of prayer. In the first, Jesus is conservative, and in the second and third he is progressive—that is, he both adopted and adapted the sacred prayer rhythms of his people.

FIRST ELEMENT: PRAY THE PSALMS

Jesus was a master of the Psalms. Wherever he heard them, in the synagogue and at the temple, he took them to heart, for the Psalms spilled constantly from his lips. Because of this, anyone who follows Jesus into the Church to pray will quickly learn that praying with Jesus means using the Psalms: His entire life was bathed with psalms.

The Beatitudes pronounced blessings on people with words taken from the psalms. Thus, we know "Blessed are the meek, for they will inherit the earth" by heart, but this is a virtual quotation from Psalm 37, which reads: "But the meek shall inherit the land, and delight themselves in abundant prosperity."

When Jesus was confronted with arguments, he responded by quoting the psalms to his verbal opponents, as in this example from the twelfth chapter of Mark, when he was pressing home the significance of his opponents' rejecting the mission God had sent him to accomplish for their benefit: "The stone that the builders rejected has become the cornerstone." This is straight from the 118th Psalm, and Jesus sees his own destiny in those words.

Just before Jesus died, he quoted directly from the twenty-second Psalm: "My God, my God, why have you forsaken me?"

When we read the Gospels, we gain the impression that the book of Psalms was one of Jesus' favorite books. How did he learn them? By participating in the synagogue. Those in attendance at synagogue were either reciting psalms or listening to psalms every week. The book of Psalms was the first teacher and the mentor in prayer for all of Judaism. So, Jesus followed the Jewish custom of learning the psalms, and he learned to make the psalms his own prayers. To adapt our image to his world, Jesus heard psalms in the basilica, and he took them with him into his *Portiuncola*, where he made them his own.

Jesus prayed psalms, and Christians have always followed his example: In the Psalms they find their own voice and they discover the voice of the Church at prayer. In an interview with Billy Graham for *USA Today* (May 15, 2005), Cathy Lynn Grossman records Billy Graham's habit of withdrawing into his own *Portiuncola* to pray psalms every day:

> His first and last words every day are prayers, and in between, prayers run like a generator in the back of his mind. "Let's just say Billy likes to stay prayed up all the time," Ross says, quoting the evangelist's longtime aide, the late T. W. Wilson.
>
> "I used to," Billy says, "read five psalms every day—that teaches me how to get along with God. Then I read a chapter of Proverbs every day and that teaches me how to get along with my fellow man."
>
> It's hard now, he says, to maintain the devotional pace that once enabled him to go through the books of Psalms and Proverbs in a month and start over again. Now, it's a psalm or two a day and proverbs as he can.

Those who familiarize themselves with the Psalms by weekly recital find a ready language for the soul. Many have read with profit *Dakota: A Spiritual Geography* by Kathleen Norris. Kathleen's own conversion story weaves in and out of retreats at Benedictine monasteries where time is structured around gathering together to recite the psalms *with* the church. The Benedictines have a motto: *"ora et labora"*—

"prayer and work." The entire day alternates between the two, as both are forms of the holy and consecrated life. As Kathleen says in her pithy language, "It may be fashionable to assert that all is holy, but not many are willing to haul ass to church four or five times a day to sing about it. It's not for the faint of heart."

After one of her retreats with the Benedictines, she relates this story, revealing that praying *with* the Church leads to a more profound ability to pray alone *in* the church.

One day in spring I left the monastery reluctantly. The winter had been hellish and I was exhausted. The last thing I wanted was a long bus ride to a conference where I'd have to be sociable. I hugged my friends good-bye, boarded the bus and collapsed into a seat. Glancing across the aisle, I was greeted by an incarnation of Psalm 131, which we'd read aloud at vespers the night before: "like a weaned child on its mother's breast, even so is my soul." A young woman, a poor young woman, to judge by her shabby clothes and traveling case, had dozed off with a small child asleep on her breast. Mother and child presented a perfect picture of peace.

Esther de Waal, an Anglican laywoman whose home is filled with kids and grandchildren, is an expert on Benedictine spirituality, the tradition devoted to reciting the entire book of Psalms weekly with the Church. In *Seeking God* she observes that the Psalms sometimes give words to her own experience, words that she cannot otherwise find.

Praying these prayers, whether alone or with the Church, she begins to sound like a psalmist:

> In the psalms I find myself at my worst and my best. Here I can acclaim God with warmth and confidence and hope, but here also I can give vent to those black thoughts that might otherwise lie hidden in the dark and angry corners of my heart. Above all the psalms express the reality of my longing for God and my joy and sufferings in the vicissitude of my search for him. Sometimes God is close, sometimes distant. I seek him in the desert and on the mountain, in poverty and in emptiness and in waiting. Today God is mindful of me, tomorrow he may not visit me. Today I am brought to the mountaintop, tomorrow I am calling from the depths. Today I am radiant, tomorrow I face darkness. Today I enjoy life, tomorrow I feel the hand of death.

The Psalms are designed for the entirety of the prayer life: They lead us out of our own personal closet to pray with others, but in praying with the Church, we hear words that lead us to pray more deeply in our own *Portiuncola*. This gives us bigger hearts as we return to the basilica. Perhaps what surprises us most as we listen carefully to the Psalms prayed in the basilica *with* the Church is how surprisingly honest and open and frank the Psalms are.

Spiritual health begins to arrive at our door when we level with God the way the Psalms do. Presbyterian pastor Mark Roberts, in Irvine, California, devoted his book on the

Psalms, *No Holds Barred: Wrestling with God in Prayer*, to honesty in prayer. Here's his graphic description:

> Our typical approach to God brings to mind Olympic wrestling, in which every move is governed by detailed rules. Our communication with God is cautious, controlled, disciplined, and relentlessly boring. Fearful that we'll do something wrong or that God won't accept our true selves, we tame our prayers to the point that we actually hide our selves from the Lord. . . . It's easy to see why even God might have trouble staying fully engaged in such a lifeless conversation. He wants us to come at him with everything we've got.

That is, God wants us to come to him with no holds barred, no rules in play. Olympic wrestling has many rules; the sort of wrestling that takes place between youngsters in the wild has no rules: The goal is to win regardless of what it takes. That, Mark Roberts is saying, is more what genuine prayer is like. Give God all you've got, and don't hold back, for only then are we being genuinely honest. The Psalms, if we listen to them intently, reveal just that kind of prayer: Don't hold back; tell God what's on your heart and in your mind.

When Jesus prayed alone or with Israel, he prayed the Psalms. The book of Psalms is the one book that joins at the hip, or should we say at the knees, the faiths of both Judaism and Christianity. The reason the two are joined by the Psalms is that psalms are the mentor for each in prayer.

That's how Jesus the Jew prayed, and that's how we also are to pray.

SECOND ELEMENT:
RECITE THE JESUS CREED

In addition to reciting and praying psalms, Jesus *adapted the* Shema *for his own followers.* When Jesus was asked which commandment was the greatest of them all, he cited two (not one): both the *Shema* from the sixth chapter of Deuteronomy and a short line from the nineteenth chapter of Leviticus. Here is Jesus' adapted *Shema*:

Hear O Israel! The Lord our God, the Lord is One. Love the Lord your God with all your heart, with all your soul, with all your mind, and with all your strength.

The second is this: Love your neighbor as yourself. There is no commandment greater than these.

If the faithful Jews around Jesus repeated the *Shema* at least twice a day, we can be sure that Jesus, too, recited it. The *Shema* was a public, communal expression of a shared story that all Jews had in common. But Jesus added to that story.

◆

"The human Jesus, as a Jew of the first century, undoubtedly joined his community in the creedal expression of the Shema."

—LUKE TIMOTHY JOHNSON, NEW TESTAMENT SCHOLAR

Though Jesus was a conservative when it came to his use of psalms, he became a bit of a progressive when it came to the *Shema*, and he began to put in place the foundation for a new sacred tradition for his followers. Jesus adopted that compressed story and adapted it: He added a new line, also from the Bible, about loving others as yourself. The earliest followers of Jesus learned to recite the *Shema* of Judaism in the enhanced form taught by Jesus (what I call "the Jesus Creed"). It was "love God" *and* "love others as yourself."

Three writers in the New Testament derive central Christian behavioral codes from the Jesus Creed itself, showing that Jesus' adaptation of the *Shema* became a compressed story for his followers. The apostle Paul, three times in the thirteenth chapter of Romans, cites "love your neighbor as yourself" and says this expresses the whole Torah. For one as committed to Torah as the apostle Paul, to say that this "love your neighbor" command expressed the whole Torah was to say a lot. James, traditionally thought to be the brother of Jesus, says in his second chapter that loving your neighbor as yourself fulfills the "royal law." The "royal law" is his term for the "capital commandment of all." And the apostle John's pen was stuck on the word "love"—over and over he uses this term in the third chapter of his first letter. Here's his basic instruction: "[T]his is the message you have heard from the beginning, that we should love one another."

These three central leaders each cited the second half of the Jesus Creed and appealed to a text that played no important role in the Jewish world before Jesus. One can

surmise that the Jesus Creed shaped early Christian thinking on how to live, and the best place for the Jesus Creed to
shape their thinking was learning to recite the Jesus Creed
throughout the day.

Put together, praying *with* Jesus and *with* the church will
mean that we learn to recite (or read) in prayer some psalms
each day and recite the Jesus Creed as well. And now we
come to the third feature of a sacred tradition established
by Jesus.

THIRD ELEMENT:
PRAY THE LORD'S PRAYER

The singular contribution of Jesus to the prayers of his people is this: He *instructed his followers to repeat the Lord's Prayer in
their sacred rhythms.* There are two versions of the Lord's
Prayer, with Matthew's version being the more familiar and
more complete one, and Luke's being less familiar and less
complete. Matthew's has seven petitions, Luke's has five.
Matthew also has a liturgical doxology (#7).

MATTHEW	LUKE
Our Father in Heaven	Father
1. Hallowed be your name.	Hallowed be your name.
2. Your kingdom come.	Your kingdom come.
3. Your will be done	
(on earth as it is in heaven)	
4. Give us this day our daily bread.	Give us each day our daily bread.

5. [F]orgive us our debts   [F]orgive us our sins
  as we also have forgiven our   for we ourselves forgive
  debtors   everyone indebted to us.
6. [D]o not bring us to the time Do not bring us to the time
  of trial, but rescue us from   of trial.
  the evil one.
[7. For yours is the kingdom,
  power, and glory, forever. Amen.
  Added later in many manuscripts.
  cf. 1 Chronicles 29:11–13.]

I have re-translated the first line introducing Luke's version of the Lord's Prayer to bring out the original, more liturgical, intent of Jesus.

Whenever you pray, you should *recite* this prayer:

Father, hallowed be your name.
Your kingdom come.
Give us each day our daily bread.
And forgive us our sins,
for we ourselves forgive everyone indebted to us.
And do not bring us to the time of trial.

This translation is rooted in the words of the Gospel of Luke itself. The original Greek for "recite" is the present imperative of "say" and it intends to command something that is to become characteristic of those who follow Jesus' words. "Whenever" his followers, as a community, prayed, they were (always) to "recite" these very words. Thus, "recite" is an accurate translation. The point I wish to make is a simple one: The Our Father prayer is to be recited *whenever Christians pray together*.

Another element of the Our Father that reveals that Jesus designed it for public recitation is that the requests are for God to give something to "us" and not to "me." Thus, we read "give *us*" and "forgive *us*" and "do not lead *us*." The only reason we have the first person plural ("us") instead of the first person singular ("me") is because the Lord's Prayer was designed for a group—the followers of Jesus—and it was designed for them to pray aloud together.

◆

Shishu Bavan *[the children's hospital founded by Mother Teresa] was a hive of activity as on any other morning. Sisters in aprons leaned over the cribs attending to the infants and children as if they were their very own. One Sister picked up a very sick baby in her arms. There seemed little hope that he would live through day. . . .*

Mother Teresa was on her way elsewhere, when she told the driver to make a detour to the children's home. As soon as the Sister saw her entering, she ran to her with the baby. Mother Teresa took the infant in her arms and quietly said the Lord's Prayer. . . .

Next day, the volunteers entered anxiously, expecting to find another occupant in the cot. They saw the same baby but it was no longer critically sick.

The Lord's Prayer is a sacred prayer for Jesus' followers, and it is especially designed by Jesus for their prayers in the basilica. The study of the earliest Christian communities confirms that they prayed this prayer as we are suggesting. By the end of the first century, the *Didache*, an early Christian writing, tells us that the Christians prayed the Lord's Prayer three times a day. The author of the *Didache* quotes the Lord's Prayer as found in Matthew's Gospel, and then says this: "Pray like this three times a day."

Here then we have a window into the "churches" of the first century. What we learn is that Jesus and his followers, nurtured as they were in the sacred rhythmical prayer of the Jewish faith, adopted the typical Jewish prayer day and adapted it into a new Christian prayer day. This day, like the Jewish tradition, is bathed in and nurtured by a regular use of the psalms as the foundation for a Christian sacred tradition of prayer, both spontaneous in a *Portiuncola* and public in the basilica: both *in* the church and *with* the Church. At the heart of a sacred tradition of praying *with* the Church is the creation of sacred rhythms at which times we pray what Jesus taught us to recite: the Psalms, the Jesus Creed, and the Lord's Prayer.

Thus, the sacred prayer tradition of Jesus is a simple adaptation of the Jewish tradition. A life of prayer rooted in the practice of Jesus and his times will involve a sacred rhythm that revolves around three or four foundational posts: the Psalms, the recitation of the Jesus Creed and the Lord's Prayer. (Some may choose to recite the Ten Commandments as well.) Incorporating these elements of a

Jesus-shaped sacred rhythm of prayer, we can now suggest a Christian prayer day.

A CHRISTIAN PRAYER DAY

Morning	Afternoon	Evening
Jesus Creed		Jesus Creed
Ten Commandments		Ten Commandments
(optional)		(optional)
Lord's Prayer	Lord's Prayer	Lord's Prayer

PERSONAL CONCLUSION

It was the discovery of these three elements in the prayer life of Jesus and the early church that convinced me—one who was reared in non-liturgical ways and one who was specifically taught in the impressionable years that reciting the Lord's Prayer in public or too often would lead to vain repetition—that I should be following Jesus out of my own *Portiuncola* to join *with* Jesus and the Church for prayers. And I was further convinced that following Jesus involved learning to pray psalms aloud with others, reciting the Jesus Creed, and constantly using the Lord's Prayer as a structure for prayer.

Ever since I came to these conclusions, I have prayed daily—two times and three times and more often than that—both the Jesus Creed (Jesus' version of the *Shema*) and the Lord's Prayer. I also regularly read quietly through two or three psalms. I do so with a prayer book. And I do these at fixed hours as often as I am able.

◆

Using [Phyllis Tickle's prayer book The] Divine Hours *has been beneficial for me in that it consistently brings me back when I find myself distracted. Specifically, praying the Lord's Prayer daily reminds me that this faith is "ours" and not just mine. I've been praying this way for several years, and my wife and I pray the compline prayers together.* —ROBERT CAMPBELL

To develop a sacred tradition of prayer is to learn to live according to a different schedule of time and to pause at fixed times to say set prayers in order to pray *with* the Church. Though sacred rhythmical prayer is not a magic potion or a simplistic solution to all of life's problems, it *is* the time-honored way Jesus taught the church to pray—to pray *with* the Church, the Church that joins to pray *with* Jesus.

PART TWO

THE CHURCH AND DAILY RHYTHMS OF PRAYER

6

PRAYER BOOKS:
A PREFACE

he foundation of praying *with* the Church is to learn to pray, as Jesus himself did, with the Psalms. The Church has learned to use psalms in a worshipful manner by organizing a reading plan for psalms, called the Psalter. Many Psalters divide up the psalms so that one can read through all of them in one month. In addition to praying with psalms, the Church has structured the reading of psalms, placing them within a time of worship by creating prayer books. Prayer books are finding their way into church and private life in new and formative ways today. Learning to pray with the Church invites us to open up these marvelous sources of devotion and allows us to pray in the manner that Jesus modeled for us.

In the next four chapters we will look at four major prayer books. *Each of these prayer books brings to life the key elements of the sacred tradition established by Jesus.* We want to look at how various Christians have fleshed out Jesus' own sacred tradition, both by adopting that sacred prayer tradition and then adapting it to their branch of the faith. First we will look at the prayer book of the Eastern Orthodox Church, then the prayer book of the Roman Catholics, then the prayer book of the Anglicans, and finally a modern, ecumenical prayer book by Phyllis Tickle. Each of these assigns a name to its prayer book: *A Manual of Eastern Orthodox Prayers, The Liturgy of the Hours, The Book of Common Prayer,* and *The Divine Hours.*

◆

Each prayer tradition has its own emphases, and the prayer books that flowed from the Reformation reflected the emphases of Calvin, Luther, Zwingli, and Menno Simons. Here is a prayer of John Calvin's, bringing to the fore his own contribution to the Reformation:

Almighty God, as nothing is better for us or more necessary for our chief happiness that to depend on thy Word, for that is a sure pledge of thy good will towards us, grant that, as thou hast favored us with so singular a benefit, we may be attentive to hear thee and submit ourselves to thee in true fear, meekness, and humility. May we be prepared in the spirit of meekness to receive whatever proceeds from thee, and may thy Word not only be precious to us, but also sweet and delightful, until we shall enjoy the perfection of that life which thine only-begotten Son has procured for us by his own blood. Amen.

WHAT IS A PRAYER BOOK?

No single definition will fit each element of each tradition's prayer book, but in essence a prayer book is *an ordering of the*

Psalms, the Lord's Prayer, and various passages of the Bible into worship.
Prayer books add short comments and worship directives
and prayers to give cohesion to the time of worship, but the
essence of a prayer book is the organization of passages
from the Bible, especially the Psalter, so that a person can
worship God and pray *with* the Church.

WHICH ONE DO I USE FIRST?

The discussion of prayer books that follows is arranged in
somewhat of a chronological order. That is, our discussion
begins with Eastern Orthodoxy's prayer book, continues on to
the classical prayer books of Roman Catholicism and of the
Anglican Communion, and then concludes with a modern
prayer book, *The Divine Hours*. This order reflects the general
view that the Orthodox order of worship is the oldest form of
worship still in practice in the Church today. However, all
the prayer books discussed in what follows are modern versions and updates of the prayer tradition of their particular
branch of the church. Roman Catholicism's magnificent *The
Liturgy of the Hours* is only a few decades old, while the
Anglican/Episcopal *The Book of Common Prayer* in use today,
although ratified in 1979, goes back centuries. So, the
chronology of the prayer books is very rough. And some
would argue that the Roman Catholic prayer tradition is older
than the Eastern Orthodox tradition. Both groups find such
debates enjoyable enough that I'll leave the debate to them.

If you have never used a prayer book, and you are
Protestant, it might be easiest to begin with Phyllis Tickle's

The Divine Hours because it is user-friendly and simpler in format. If you are Orthodox, *A Manual of Eastern Orthodox Prayers*, with its single set of morning and evening prayers may be the simplest format available, though it lacks the variety many people look for. If you are Roman Catholic, or if you would like to see what the Roman Catholic prayer book tradition looks like, begin with *The Glenstal Book of Prayer: A Benedictine Prayer Book*. This prayer book contains one week of morning and evening prayers, which can be repeated from week to week; it also contains some other useful prayers and is small enough to use when one is traveling.

◆

I find The Liturgy of the Hours *and* Celtic Daily Prayer *and* The Divine Hours *to be incredibly useful. I think much of "spontaneous prayer" in my life turned into meaningless recitation—it was unfocused and therefore a very unhealthy prayer life. So, the discipline of fixed prayers and joining with the church universal, along with the help of liturgy, the careful weaving of tradition, reading Scripture, and the community of faith have deepened me—as God has grown my heart, my character, and my actions into a form that is more reflective of Jesus.* —DOUG JONES

There are other easily accessible prayer books. One is *Celtic Daily Prayer: From the Northumbria Community;* it is easy to use and, like *The Divine Hours*, it has plenty of variety.

Another is *The Little Book of Hours: Praying with the Community of Jesus;* this Christian community on Cape Cod is devoted to the sacred prayer rhythms and traditions, and this little book is the result of mature thinking and practice.

Over time, many (and I am included among these) will want to put down their first prayer book, whether it is *The Divine Hours* or *The Glenstal Book of Payer* or *Celtic Daily Prayer*, so they can explore more deeply other prayer book traditions that pause at fixed times to pray with the Church. Start where you prefer to start. Experiment with various prayer books. Try to use one for at least a month in order to let its rhythms become obvious to you. In each you will be drawn to see the wisdom of both sacred rhythms and sacred prayers for praying with the Church.

◆

It would be rare to find a single bookstore that carried each of the prayer books, so let me suggest you try them online. There is a link to prayer books on my Blog site (www.jesuscreed.org). On that page's right-hand sidebar you will find "Daily Prayers" and a link to each of the major prayer books. The Eastern Orthodox prayer book is not, to my knowledge, fully available online, but you will find a link to the Web site of the Orthodox Church in America, and there one can find Morning Prayers and Evening Prayers.

THE CHURCH CALENDAR

Prayer books are shaped by the Church calendar, and their themes and readings and prayers are shaped by those events. Here are the seasons and their emphases:

Advent	*Longing for the Messiah*
Christmas	*Celebration of the Messiah*
Epiphany (and after)	*Commitment to the Messiah's manifestation*
Lent	*Repentance and Renewal*
The Great Triduum*	*Fasting, prayer, and commitment*
Easter to Pentecost	*Die to sin, rise to new life in the Spirit*
After Pentecost	*Deepening the gospel, theology, and living*

* Maundy Thursday, Good Friday, Paschal Vigil

The Church calendar enables us to relive the gospel drama year after year so that its central themes are woven, like the infinite cord of the Celtic way, deeply into the fabric of our life together and our lives apart. The only way to let the spirituality of the Church calendar work its way into our soul is to join *with* the Church in prayer and worship. If you use any of the prayer books, this calendrical work will be done for you—and you will be invited in the prayer books to pray *with* the Church.

◆

Through the discipline of the Christian year we can experience the power of Christ within the community of the church, through its worship and in our lives twenty-four hours a day, seven days a week.

Almighty God, unto whom all hearts are open, all desires known, and from whom no secrets are hid: cleanse the thoughts of my heart by the inspiration of your Holy Spirit, that I may perfectly love you and worthily magnify your holy name by the practice of Christian-year spirituality; through Jesus Christ my Lord. Amen.

—ROBERT WEBBER

If you open up a typical prayer book, such as *The Book of Common Prayer*, which we will look at in chapter nine, you will find a Psalter. Here are two lines from Psalm 121:

I lift up my eyes to the hills;*
from where is my help to come?

The older version of *The Book of Common Prayer* used Coverdale's translation:

I will lift up mine eyes unto the hills;*
from whence cometh my help?

Those of us nurtured in the days when the King James Version was *the* Protestant Bible find nostalgia and poetry in a translation like Coverdale's, but my point concerns the asterisk (*). The asterisk is a notation for those who chant or sing the psalm.

By the time of Jesus, Israelites didn't just read the psalms; they learned to "sing" or "chant" them. That is because the poetic nature of the psalms brought out a poetic form for public, communal reading. In fact, in the fifth chapter of the letter to the Ephesians, Paul says this: "as you sing psalms and hymns and spiritual songs among yourselves." That is, the early Christians typically sang psalms. We now call the singing or chanting of the psalms "psalmody." Many saints have followed Augustine's oft-quoted observation: "Whoever sings the psalms, prays twice." The singing of psalms together, in other words, deepens the reading of the psalms.

◆

"It's striking to think that the hymn that, according to Matthew's Gospel, Jesus and his friends sang after the Last Supper was perhaps something a bit like Gregorian chant. The chant is a kind of plainsong, the predominant musical form in the early church, which consists of only one melody line, with no descants or counterpoints. It is a simple form of music, one that pretty much anyone could join in; but its simplicity is also deliberate, part of its meditative nature. The songs were intended to set the texts, biblical and otherwise, that were being sung, and to focus the mind on their meaning. In other words, this kind of singing was central to the liturgy, the services that were being held in Christian churches; and the singing was an integral element in the creation of the beautiful, spiritual atmosphere that Christians sought."

—JONATHAN HILL

Psalmody has taken on four forms, and the asterisk is the clue for each of them. First, some churches simply read the entire psalm aloud, merely pausing each time they come to an asterisk. Second, some read psalms *antiphonally*: One person or group reads the first line, and another person or group reads the second line (the asterisk being the clue when to change readers). Third, some read psalms *responsorially*: Here the above two lines (or maybe some more) are read by a solo voice (usually a talented one) and the choir or congregation then reads a short line taken from that psalm that is repeated each time the solo voice pauses. Fourth, many congregations read the Psalter *responsively*: The minister or liturgist reads one line and the congregation reads the other line.

Psalmody reached its apex, according to many, in the Benedictine chant. For the Benedictines the asterisk not only indicates a pause or a change of readers but also a change of tone, up one note or down one note, something the Benedictines have also mastered. This form of psalmody is aesthetically beautiful and has the capacity to draw both chanter and listener into another level of worship.

THE SIGN OF THE CROSS

Some prayer books note when a person is to make the sign of the cross. The prayer book has a small cross in the text (+) to indicate the moment for crossing oneself. Protestants have avoided signing themselves, mostly in protest of the Roman Catholic tradition. But, as I have told my Protestant students for years, the sign of the cross is no more Roman Catholic than a sermon is Protestant. Christians have crossed themselves from the earliest days. Tertullian, as a powerful apologist for the Christian faith in the late second and early third centuries, said this:

> At every forward step and movement,
> at every going in and out [this echoes the Shema],
> when we put on our clothes and shoes,
> when we bathe,
> when we sit at table,
> when we light the lamps,
> on couch,
> on seat,
> in all the ordinary actions of daily life,
> we trace upon the forehead the sign [of the Cross].

◆

The Celtic Daily Prayer *order for Morning Prayer begins with this:*

+ In the name of the Father,

and of the Son,

and of the Holy Spirit. Amen.

The Eastern Orthodox have a custom for doing this—head to heart, and then right shoulder to left shoulder—while the Western Church (including Roman Catholics) have a different custom—from head to heart, and then left shoulder to right shoulder. Either way, the sign of the cross is made.

In the prayer book traditions, both the Eastern and Western churches have asked Christians to begin the session by "signing" themselves. I have for years made the sign of the cross (in the Eastern fashion), and I do so simply to remind myself of the centrality of the Cross in personal life and prayer.

A REMINDER

Prayer books are not intended to be an alternative to spontaneous prayers. Each of us has our own *Portiuncola* where we can pray alone *in* the church, and each of us is summoned into the larger basilica to pray *with* the Church. Prayer books are helpful for both kinds of prayer—both for time alone and for time together.

Prayer books, along with the psalms, are our mentors as we learn how to pray. Each prayer book is shaped by a specific theological tradition, and each of us is probably more comfortable with one tradition rather than with the prayer books from other traditions. The aim of this book is to invite you to join other Christians in praying *with* the Church by learning how to pray using the prayer books of other traditions.

7

HOW THE EASTERN ORTHODOX PRAY WITH THE CHURCH

In *Facing East*, the book mapping her conversion to Eastern Orthodoxy, Frederica Mathewes-Green opens up her home for us in the early hours of the morning when, so she tells us, her body routinely wakens and can't find sleep. When this happens, it is her practice to retire to her study. There she finds a comfortable place, quiets herself, and prays. Here is what she says, and she tells us that she recites this one-line prayer until her body tells her it is time to go back to sleep:

Lord Jesus Christ, be merciful to me.

"The goal," she says, "is to focus on those recurring words, not on any other prayers or intercessions, not on Bible study or theological truths; you have all day long for that. For this half hour, just fall into the presence of God like warming your hands before a fire, without a conscious thought in your head."

I know the experience of routinely waking at night and not being able to fall back asleep, and I know the experience of lying there and finding myself praying prayers that others in the church use. But what Frederica prays is singularly Eastern Orthodox. Called the "Jesus Prayer," the line "be merciful to me" is taken from a parable of Jesus found in Luke's eighteenth chapter. Over and over she recites the Jesus Prayer. She describes, in true Orthodox fashion, how she has learned to pray this prayer in accordance with her heartbeats: one word for each beat of the heart. Lord. Jesus. Christ. Have mercy. On me. Over and over. Sometimes she gets distracted, but always she strives for focused attention on the words of that prayer in tune with the beat of the heart.

This prayer joins her with millions of (mostly Orthodox) Christians who for centuries have dedicated themselves to the Lord throughout the day by reciting this prayer.

The practice of reciting a single prayer over and over throughout the day for Orthodox Christians was not an invention of the church, for the *Shema* itself ("Hear O Israel! . . . Love the Lord thy God . . .") was to be said when retiring and awaking, when leaving home and entering home, and when traveling—it was both a summary of the Torah and a companion for the journey. As such it could be repeated as often as one liked. The *Shema* was (and still is) an all-day reminder, not just a twice-a-day routine.

I have been reciting the Jesus Creed (not the Jesus Prayer) for several years throughout the day, and not just at fixed times.

Hear O Israel! The Lord our God, the Lord is One. Love the Lord your God with all your heart, with all your soul, with all your mind, and with all your strength. And the second is this: Love your neighbor as yourself. There is no commandment greater than these.

This set prayer has become my travel companion and sacred rhythmical prayer—when I commute, when I walk around the lake in the evening with Kris, when I am passing from class to class, when I am eating lunch by myself, when I drink tea or coffee. It has entwined itself into the fabric of my day, my life; in fact, my very being. It is not magic and it is not a talisman; it is simply a way I constantly communicate with God and bring myself into God's presence. Some days I say it fifty or more times; some days not nearly so often. Rarely do I go an hour without reciting it.

What the Jesus Creed is to me, the Jesus Prayer been for centuries to the Orthodox Church. It centers one's life. But another dimension that is the focus of this book is that by reciting such prayers we join in praying *with* the Church. Others are also reciting prayers, others are centering themselves on God, and by reciting such prayers we join them in the great basilica called the communion of the saints.

Using our "spare time" for such prayers is not an obsession but a way of centering our lives on God with others. Sometimes we best come to realize the importance of centering our whole being before God because of what the absence of centering does to us. None has said this better than the Orthodox theologian Alexander Schmemann. In his *Journal* for November 28, 1973, he divulged what being busy and fussing about his leadership roles were doing to his spirit. Here is how he put it:

I long to be free, free to "live": my wife and family (no time), friends (no time), nature (no time), cultural reading (no leisure). I would like to live in such a way that every particle of time would be fullness (and not fuss); and being full, time would be prayer, a tie, a relationship with God, transparency for God who gave us life, not fuss.

Why? "There is," Schmemann later says, "undoubtedly only one joy: to know Him and share Him with each other." The Jesus Prayer (and the Jesus Creed) and the prayer book traditions are designed for just this: "to know Him and share Him *with each other*."

Eastern Orthodoxy has a singular theme in all of its teaching about prayer: Union with God is the final goal of human existence. All of the prayer traditions, not the least of which is the Jesus Prayer, focus on this goal. By turning our hearts to God, whether alone in our own *Portiuncola* or with others in the church, we are joining ourselves together to strive for union with God.

The Orthodox remind us of a central truth about prayer: The purpose of prayer is not to get good at it, but for the Church to become good through it. And the Church becomes good by utilizing set prayers at set times. The Orthodox use both the Jesus Prayer and, as we will show later, in this chapter, a special prayer book.

THE JESUS PRAYER:
AN OLD PRAYER STILL IN USE

Historians of the Church know that from the fourth century on there has been evidence of the use of reciting the name of Jesus in a one-word (*monologistic*) prayer—simply saying prayerfully the name of Jesus. The Western theologian St. Augustine wrote of "the name [of Jesus] that is so dear to us, so sweet to pronounce." Well before Augustine and clearly after his time, many Christians added other words, and many preferred the words of the tax collector in the parable of Jesus: "God, be merciful to me, a sinner!"

Within a few centuries after the time of Christ it was also clear that a special prayer was being said by many Eastern Christians, and that prayer is now called the Jesus Prayer or sometimes the Prayer of the Heart (because it is said in tune with the heartbeat). This prayer is prominent in *The Manual of Eastern Orthodox Prayers*, the Orthodox prayer book. After making the sign of the cross in Morning Prayers, the Orthodox begin with this:

God, be merciful to me, a sinner.

The Jesus Prayer is nothing more than an adaptation of these words from the parable.

The Orthodox have always been flexible, so the basic shape of the prayer has itself changed—and each of us is encouraged to adapt it for ourselves—but it is a prayer that unites many in the Orthodox tradition. So, here are some of the many forms of the Jesus Prayer, with some others saying (as does Frederica in the example above) "have mercy" instead of "be merciful":

Jesus.

Lord Jesus.

Lord Jesus Christ.

Lord Jesus Christ, Son of God.

Lord Jesus Christ, Son of God, be merciful to me.

Lord Jesus Christ, Son of God, be merciful to me, a sinner.

Lord Jesus Christ, be merciful to me a sinner.

Lord Jesus Christ, be merciful to me.

Lord Jesus Christ, be merciful.

Lord Jesus, be merciful.

Jesus, be merciful.

The Jesus Prayer is an element of what is called "hesy-chasm," or the pursuit of silence before God—silence to recollect one's heart before God, silence to give one's full attention to the prayer itself, and silence to hear from God. It is the silence of centering on God. Within Orthodoxy, the Jesus Prayer finds its proper context not so much in public liturgy but in the private, silent devotion of ordinary living. Prayer for the Orthodox, as for Israel and Jesus and the entire church, is both private and communal. The Jesus Prayer takes the tax collector's prayer and adapts it for private use.

This prayer has been adapted by more than the Eastern Orthodox, even if it remains singularly Eastern. Evelyn Underhill, an Anglican, in her well-known book *Worship*, recommends that Christians say the Jesus Prayer. And an emerging church leader in the USA, Tony Jones, devotes an entire chapter in his book on spiritual practices from various Christian traditions, *The Sacred Way*, to the Jesus Prayer. In fact, he confesses this: "[T]he Jesus Prayer has become very significant to me, maybe more than any practice I've investigated, and it's an important party of my Rule of Life."

While the Jesus Prayer often functions as a personal, private prayer, in using this prayer the Christian at the same time joins millions in the church who use the same prayer. It is, then, both a personal and a communal prayer.

HOW TO SAY THE JESUS PRAYER

This is not a comprehensive book on spiritual practices or on the Christian life, but instead on the value of set prayers at fixed times, both in the context of praying alone *in* the church and praying together *with* the Church. The Jesus Prayer is one such set prayer that can be used, like the *Shema* or the Jesus Creed, by all Christians. Some experiment with the Jesus Prayer, and put it aside; others find in the Jesus Prayer a way to focus all their spiritual attention. With practice, this prayer can become a source of spiritual formation as we journey together in the path God has for each of us.

None tells us how to use the Jesus Prayer better than the anonymous Pilgrim, the seeker at the center of the nineteenth-century Eastern Orthodox spiritual classic *The Way of the Pilgrim*. This Pilgrim is on an odyssey across Russia with only a knapsack and inside it only dry crusts of bread and a Holy Bible. Entering a church on the twenty-fourth Sunday after Pentecost, he hears the following statement of the apostle

Paul being read in the scriptural reading: "Pray constantly." Pilgrim goes on a quest to discover what it can mean to pray constantly. An elderly spiritual advisor, what Orthodox Russians call a *staretz*, teaches the Pilgrim that the wise in the church have learned to pray constantly by reciting the Jesus Prayer ("Lord Jesus Christ, have mercy on me!"). Then he teaches the Pilgrim about the profound spirituality that comes from the Eastern Orthodox four-volume spiritual classic, the *Philokalia* (pronounced "fil-o-ka-LEE-a").

The mentor reads to the Pilgrim from the *Philokalia* the words of St. Simeon the New Theologian, words that continue to shape the Eastern Orthodox and many Protestants and Roman Catholics to this day: "Sit alone and in silence; bow your head and close your eyes; relax your breathing and with your imagination look into your heart; direct your thoughts from your head into your heart. And while inhaling say, 'Lord Jesus Christ, have mercy on me,' either softly with your lips or in your mind. Endeavor to fight distractions but be patient and peaceful and repeat this process frequently." As St. John of Climacus put it in the seventh century: "May the remembrance of Jesus be united to your breathing." In this way the person praying joins the church in prayer.

◆

The physical or psychosomatic element of the Jesus Prayer became very important to some and for others it was unhealthy to emphasize coordinating breathing and pulse to the prayer. Eventually the

Orthodox "drew swords" over it: St. Gregory Palamas weighed in against Barlaam the Calabrian, an opponent of the breathing-praying rhythm or the physical component of this prayer. Gregory argued that connecting the prayer to the rhythms of the body expressed more completely the belief in Jesus as the Incarnation of God's Word. By letting one's spirit come into complete harmony with one's body, the union of Christ's own two natures—human and divine—came into focus. The Pilgrim himself would have known this from the Philokalia. *Whether or not those today who use the Jesus Prayer are aware of this debate hardly matters, but the connection of the body and the spirit is a dimension of spirituality that is on the rise in many Christian circles today.*

Like many who try to use the Jesus Prayer today, this Pilgrim also struggled with distractions. So the elderly advisor told Pilgrim to recite the prayer aloud. Then he instructed him to say it 3,000 times a day, something he found easier on the third day. Then the elder instructed him to up the number to 6,000 and then again to 12,000 times a day. And then it took hold of his entire being.

The elder then gave him the wisdom he needed: "You may recite the Prayer as many times as you wish; call on the name of Jesus all your waking moments, without counting, and humbly resign yourself to God's will expecting help from Him." The rest of *The Way of the Pilgrim* is a compelling story of the spiritual power of the Pilgrim as he wanders from place to place, at peace with God, and spreading the joy of the kingdom to all who would listen to him tell his story of the Jesus Prayer.

USING THE JESUS PRAYER TODAY

Eastern Orthodoxy has a rich prayer tradition, the Jesus Prayer being but one example. For those who would like to join the Orthodox in the basilica, learning to recite the Jesus Prayer will make their company easier.

How do we do use the Jesus Prayer and do so in such a way that we are consciously joining the church in prayer? First, we focus our thoughts; second, we pause in silent reverence; third, we say the Jesus Prayer gently and slowly in rhythm with our breathing and our heartbeats. And, fourth, we are conscious at some level that we are joining brothers and sisters all around the globe who have made the Jesus Prayer their special prayer.

The wisdom of the experienced is this: This prayer has the capacity to sustain one's spiritual life, focused as it is on Jesus Christ and our own need of mercy, and it has the ability to work its way into our very being. Those who use this prayer as their daily guide witness that their very breathing and their very heartbeats become prayers themselves.

The significance of this element of Eastern Orthodox prayer is worth pausing to consider: By reciting the Jesus Prayer, all those who join this distinctly Orthodox form of spirituality place Jesus Christ at their very center. As we will see below, other elements of the faith are brought to bear in Orthodox prayers, but at this point it needs to be emphasized that Jesus comes to the fore through this prayer. What we learn here for the development of praying *with* the Church is that every minute of every day can become tuned into the presence of Jesus Christ if we discipline ourselves to spend a concentrated period on a set prayer. As we pray this prayer, we join throngs of others who are devoted to such a prayer rhythm.

PRAY IN THE MORNING AND THE EVENING

The Orthodox sacred tradition developed out of the ancient Jewish recitation of the *Shema* and the early Christian recitation of the Lord's Prayer. At times, Pilgrim speaks of rising to say his prayers, and it is most likely that he is here referring to the set prayers that the Eastern Orthodox have written for both morning and evening prayer. Along with the use of the Psalms and the Jesus Prayer, which every Christian tradition uses in its prayer books, and the use of icons for worship, the Orthodox have produced out of their nearly two millennia of thinking and practice some of the church's best-known prayers.

Like the two great Western church traditions—the Roman Catholic and the Protestant—the Eastern Orthodox Church has developed set prayers for both morning and evening. *A Manual of Eastern Orthodox Prayers* summons each of us from our own *Portiuncola* into the wider church for both morning and evening prayers. The *Manual* is designed to be used together with a lectionary that guides the

Orthodox reading of the Bible. A good Orthodox source for daily Scripture readings is the Web site http://www.oca.org/Reading.asp.

I struggle with the *Manual's* morning and evening prayer because the prayers are the same for every day of the year. But, I'll also thank the Orthodox for giving to us some of the most theologically studied prayers in the history of the church. Their prayer tradition is a never-ending source, a well in which we sense we are touching bottom, but the waters continually replenish themselves.

Nicolas Zernov, the original editor of the *Manual*, tells us that three benefits come to those who learn to pray *with* the Church using this *Manual*. First, Christians who use the *Manual* train themselves in the "best tradition of prayer." Second, they keep a bond of unity with other Eastern Orthodox Christians—and for a Protestant like me the *Manual* permits me to join with them in my prayer life. And third, these prayers sustain a Christian during dry and depressing times in life. I wish more people knew the truth of this claim. Reciting the wise prayers of the church "warms the cold heart, strengthens the weakened will, and brings the individual into that fellowship of prayer which binds together all the members of the mystical Body of Christ." Some Christians find themselves so dry in their own *Portiuncolas* that the only prayers that make sense to them are the prayers they recite in the larger basilica, the prayers they utter with other brothers and sisters in the Church.

◆

The most important thing [about praying with prayer books] is it helps me be intentional about being in the presence of God all day long. The next most important thing is the petition aspects of my personal prayer have been much more organized and focused, as well as more open to how I think the Holy Spirit wants me to pray. The well-thought-out, time-tested structure has really enabled me to pray on a daily basis—I simply couldn't sustain that beyond a couple of months previously. —DANA AMES

I know this myself. Some days I don't feel like praying or I find my own spontaneous prayers to be worn down. I've found on such days that the prayer books and praying with the Church can suddenly enliven my own prayers and make suggestions for things to pray about that I had long forgotten, and that they can drive me back to my own *Portiuncola* with renewed energy for personal prayer.

THE GENIUS OF EASTERN PRAYERS

The Eastern prayer tradition evokes several rich themes in prayer. These emphases are largely lost in some sectors of the church, and familiarity with the *Manual* can bring these important concerns back to the surface for us. Zernov brings out three of them in one sentence: "an acute realization of man's enslavement to sin, a deep sense of the Divine majesty and glory, and the frequent references to the

Mother of God." He's right: If one reads prayerfully through the morning and evening prayers one finds an emphasis on our sin, and our sin is set in powerful contrast with God's glory and majesty. Hence, the Orthodox emphasize the importance of God's goodness and grace in their prayers. And the presence of Mary in many of the prayers is especially notable. While it will be easier for Roman Catholics to join hands with the Eastern Orthodox in prayers addressed to Mary, some Protestants may struggle here.

◆

Here's a Protestant who writes of his encounter with Mary in the Eastern prayer tradition: Some time ago I was introduced to The Agpeya, *the Coptic Orthodox version of the hours of prayer by a Coptic priest, and I have been using it ever since. It takes a little getting used to culturally, as it is longer and much more repetitive than Western versions, plus there are prayers to Mary and the Saints which I'm fine with but may bother some of a strict evangelical/reformed bent. I found it a challenge to learn and practice the full version, but it's very much worth the effort. Apart from anything else it has an Eastern flavor and makes much greater use of the psalms than the Western version, [something] I suspect is much closer to the kinds of regular prayers used by the Jews at the time of Jesus.* —SHAWN HERLES

As an outsider to the Eastern prayer tradition, I would add yet another that Zernov does not mention: the Trinitarian nature of Eastern prayers. Over and over lines are said three times, the Trinity is mentioned, and one comes into regular contact with the theological orthodoxy that makes Christianity what it is: a view that God is One and Three at the same time.

The Morning Prayer tradition begins with this:

When you awake, before you begin the day, stand with reverence before the All-Seeing God. Make the Sign of the Cross and say:

In the Name of the Father, and of the Son, and of the Holy Ghost. Amen.

There are other forms of Eastern Orthodox prayers, but they all begin with some kind of invocation of the Trinity.

I have mentioned that I was reared in the low-low church tradition where we did not recite prayers repetitively in public—and neither did we ever confess our sins together— as individuals or as a body. The Eastern Orthodox *Manual* will hear none of this: Confession of sin is inherent to what it means for a Christian to worship, and so confession is found on every page. If you want to learn how to work confession of sin into your sacred rhythms, there is no better source than the Eastern prayer tradition.

One who uses the morning prayer from *A Manual of Eastern Orthodox Prayers* will not only begin each day with the sign of the cross and an invocation of the Trinity, but will next say this: God, be merciful to me, a sinner. And then there follows a prayer to the Holy Spirit:

O Heavenly King, O Comforter, the Spirit of truth, who are everywhere and fillest all things, the treasure of blessings, and giver of life, come and abide in us.

In truth Orthodox fashion, the next sentence brings back the matter of sin:

Cleanse us from all impurity, and of thy goodness save our souls.

I've asked my Eastern Orthodox colleague Bradley Nassif if there is not too much of this sin orientation in the Orthodox prayer book. He thinks not. Perhaps we Protestants, he suggests, need to listen a little more to the Orthodox themes of prayer.

EXAMPLES FROM A MANUAL OF EASTERN ORTHODOX PRAYERS

Like Roman Catholics, the Eastern Orthodox use aids to prayer, the two most notable of which are the use of the sign of the cross and the use of a prayer rope marked with notches—and one moves from one notch to the other as one proceeds through one's prayers. Whenever I use the Orthodox prayer *Manual*, I cross myself at the appropriate times—and probably at inappropriate times, too!

Our first encounter with Orthodox *Manual* may lead to frustration for the non-Orthodox. It is our lack of familiarity with the prayers and not what is being said and prayed that makes the Orthodox prayer tradition seem distant to those of us who are not Orthodox. Yet, of all the prayer books, the Eastern *Manual* might be the simplest because it does not change from day to day. A day or two with the *Manual* will give any Christian dedicated to learning to pray with the Church, alongside the Orthodox, enough time to understand both the meaning and genius of the Orthodox prayer tradition. With a little patience and a little trial and error, and maybe a few questions for an Orthodox friend, the Eastern Orthodox prayer tradition can become a source of light for our journey together (even if we stand in different parts of the basilica at times).

The morning prayer begins, as I have stated above, on a Trinitarian note with a confession of sin. There are other elements to the morning prayer that deserve mention. The Orthodox prayer tradition has standard names for certain prayers, and one of its better known ones is the *Trisagion*, the "thrice-holy" prayer:

Holy God, Holy and Mighty, Holy Immortal, have mercy on us (this is to be said three times, for each person of the Trinity).

And the prayer tradition all comes together in the prayer to the Holy Trinity:

Most Holy Trinity, have mercy upon us.
O Lord, cleanse us from our sins.
O Master, pardon our iniquities.
O Holy One, visit and heal our infirmities for thy Name's sake.
Lord, have mercy. Lord, have mercy. Lord, have mercy.
Glory be to the Father, and to the Son, and to the Holy Ghost, both
now and ever, and unto the ages of ages. Amen.

Next comes the Lord's Prayer, short hymns to the Trinity, St. Basil's prayer to the Trinity, Psalm 51 (confession of sins once again), The Creed, four prayers by St. Makarios the Great (d. 390), another prayer of St. Basil, a prayer to the guardian angel, a prayer to the Mother of God, an invocation in praise of "your saint," another hymn to the Mother of God, a hymn to the day's feast (and there are lots of these, too), and then prayers for the living and dead, and a conclusion.

If, after seeing all those prayers and names, you're lost, it may be because you didn't grow up in the Eastern tradition. But, let this be said, there is nothing complex or tricky here. In fact, the Eastern prayer tradition is simple and is perhaps the oldest prayer tradition in the Church. (For some, what is oldest is best.) To begin, pick up one of the various editions of the Eastern morning prayer tradition or go to a Web site where the morning prayer is offered, such as this one:http://www.oca.org/OCSelect-Prayer.asp?SID=2& name=Morning%20Prayers

The evening prayer tradition is similar to that of the morning, with similar emphases.

SPECIAL PRAYERS

Other than the Jesus Prayer, perhaps what is most notable about the Eastern prayer book is the rich storehouse of prayers for special occasions. One of these prayers struck me one evening after I was watching a political fracus on the news. It is called "Prayers for our Enemies." (I thought some of the politicians involved would do well to begin their day or end their day with this prayer.) There are two parts, the *Troparion* and the *Kontakion*. These terms refer to the theme of the prayer and its response.

Troparion

Thou who didst pray for them that crucified thee, O Lord, Lover of the souls of men, and who didst command thy servants to pray for their enemies, forgive those who hate and maltreat us, and turn our lives from all harm and evil to brotherly love and good works: for this we humbly bring our prayer, that with one accord and one heart we may glorify thee who alone lovest mankind.

Kontakion

As thy first martyr Stephen prayed to thee for his murderers, O Lord, so we fall before thee and pray: forgive all who hate and maltreat us and let not one of them perish because of us, but all be saved by thy grace, O God the all-bountiful.

These prayers move me. In fact, those who find it in themselves to pray such prayers for their enemies may find fewer and fewer enemies and more and more friends to stand alongside with in prayer!

How do we begin our day? The Orthodox have a prayer that can help us surrender our day to the wondrous, if not always known, will of God. It comes from Metropolitan Philaret, from Moscow, and dates to the middle of the nineteenth century:

O Lord, grant me to greet the coming day in peace, help me in all things to rely upon your holy will. In every hour of the day reveal your will to me. Bless my dealings with all who surround me. Teach me to treat all that comes to me throughout the day with peace of soul and with firm conviction that your will governs all. In all my deeds and words, guide my thoughts and feelings. In unforeseen events, let me not forget that all are sent by you. Teach me to act firmly and wisely, without embittering and embarrassing others. Give me strength to bear the fatigue of the coming day with all that it shall bring. Direct my will, teach me to pray. And you, yourself, pray in me. Amen.

The *Manual*, along with other Orthodox prayer books, contains prayers for many occasions. While many of these are used by individuals, whenever we pick up a written prayer, we become conscious that we are not only praying alone, but we are also praying with the Church.

WHAT CAN I DO WITH THE *MANUAL?*

It is wise for Christians, of whatever stripe and faith, to familiarize themselves with the great prayer books of the Church, not only because we come into contact with prayers well stated, but also because we come into contact with our brothers and sisters throughout the world. Not only now, but through all the ages.

I sometimes jokingly tell my Protestant students that when we get to heaven the first thing we will have to do is learn the prayer books of the Orthodox and the Roman Catholics. "Why?" they often ask. "Because," I reply, "those are the prayers they know, and we'll be asked to join in with them during prayer meetings." Such quips, of course, don't tell the whole truth—but neither are they falsehoods.

If we are going to leave our own little *Portiuncolas* to pray *with* the Church, the best place to begin after learning the Psalter is to become familiar with the prayer books of the rest of the Church. *A Manual of Eastern Orthodox Prayers* is a good place to begin if we wish to stand in the Orthodox section of the Church to pray with our sisters and brothers.

8

HOW THE ROMAN CATHOLICS PRAY WITH THE CHURCH

n June of 2005, Kris and I spent ten gloriously beautiful days in Italy. We meandered through the ruins of Rome and walked where Cicero walked, we loved the gentle hills filled with olives and grapes around the flat plains in Umbria, and we schlepped up and down Assisi's hills and spent quiet times in the pinkish churches of Assisi.

We also spent some time in Nursia, home of St. Benedict, author of the guide for Western monasticism that is put into practice by so many today: *The Rule of St. Benedict*. We entered Nursia through the Porta Romana, a large pinkish gate bearing the words VETVSTA NVRSIA ("Ancient Nursia"). We ambled down the main street, Corso Setorio, absorbing the sounds and smells of this ancient Italian village. At one spot we entered a shop that sold breads, grains, and cheeses, and the smell of the cheese molds were so piercing Kris had to exit and stood outside—I took in some deep drafts and they smelled deeply of the history of Nursia. The shop carried the foods that have sustained Nursia for centuries, and some of them, perhaps (so Kris thought), were from the time of Benedict himself.

We walked a few more blocks and came upon Piazza San Benedetto, named after St. Benedict. We then crossed the piazza to the Basilica di San Benedetto. It was early, so we entered the basilica and realized that we were all alone in this historic church. The smell of incense, so typical of Italian churches, filled the air. More important, what also filled the air were the gloriously capacious tones of the Benedictine monks singing the church service, or "office," at the hour of terce—roughly 9 AM. The monks were situated somewhere below the first floor, and terce was not open to the public, but the monks' voices filled the basilica and transformed it into sounds that evoked worship. We were treated to a concert all by ourselves. More accurately, it was a concert of the church at prayer, and we were treated to a front row seat.

I've been blessed to hear lots of good Christian music over the years, and my college has made something of a name for itself with its musical talent, but there is nothing quite like the tone of Benedictine monks singing in a cool, gray medieval basilica filled with incense and empty of tourists. I don't know Latin well enough to have understood all the words, but I did recognize some words from the Psalter, from the long 119th psalm: "Lord, how I love your law! It is ever in my mind." It is Benedictine to sing, and it is also typically Benedictine to sing that particular psalm.

BENEDICT OF NURSIA

Benedict was born in AD 480 and baptized in the small church that existed at this very same location. Benedict founded the monastic order that transformed the monasteries of Europe. As Norvene Vest has observed in her edition of *The Rule of St. Benedict*: "Benedict was not particularly a theoretician. He loved God, he believed Christian life was best lived in community, and he sought practical ways to guide the brothers under his care in the daily life of holiness." Benedict believed that all of life was holy, and that it was possible for monks to follow Jesus Christ in his way of life. And ever since Benedict's time, ordinary Christian folk have successfully followed his way of life as well.

At the heart of his Order was devotion to the hours of prayer as an act of praying *with* the Church. These separate hours of prayer are often called "offices." "Offices" comes from the Latin *officium*, which means "duty." Benedict, adapting the models available to him at his time, outlined the time of day for each office and which psalms were most appropriate for that time of day. Those who follow Benedict's *Rule* begin their day of prayer (either at night, at the office of vigils, or in the morning prayer office, called lauds) with Psalm 95. The hours of prayer as outlined by Benedict promote personal spiritual formation, but that formation falls, like breezes from a mountain, from the communal experience of praying with the Church.

This deep Church tradition of the hours of prayer, if one begins to live within its sacred time rhythms, functions as a protest against the busyness of a world enthralled by work and money and the relentless pursuit of the time clock. Here, in contrast, we find a day punctuated by prayer and worship.

◆

"For this reason," says Francis in The Rule *of 1221, "all the friars, whether clerics or laics, are to say the divine office, the praises and prayers, according to what they are assigned to say." (Chapter 3.3)*

Devotion to the hours or offices is the duty of those who undertake to live according to *The Rule of St. Benedict*—no one has to. Christians who use set prayers in the morning and the evening may not know that they are praying psalms in a manner established many centuries ago by the Benedictine pattern of prayer.

HOURS OF PRAYER

Benedict established seven hours of prayer during the day and one at night; collectively they are known as "the Divine Office" or simply "the hours":

TRADITIONAL NAME	NAME OF OFFICE	TODAY TIME
Vigils (or Matins)	Office of Readings	Midnight
Lauds	**Morning Prayer**	6 AM–11 AM
(Prime)	(No longer generally used)	(6 AM–7 AM)

Traditional Name	Name of Office	Today Time
Terce	Midmorning Prayer	9 AM
Sext	Midday Prayer	Noon
None (rhymes with "tone")	Midafternoon Prayer	3 PM
Vespers	**Evening Prayer**	3 PM–6 PM
Compline	Night Prayer	Before bed

Praying at fixed times was not new to Benedict—it is as old as the psalmists. Nor was the use of the Psalter a Benedictine innovation. Already by the first generation, Christians were using the Psalter for prayers. Nor was the commitment to praying through the entire Psalter every month new. Rather, Benedict's contribution lay in his charismatic leadership and guidance of the monks around him. The pattern of prayers that he established became the model for future generations of the church. In one way or another Benedict's model is still used by millions of Christians—Roman Catholic, Eastern Orthodox, and Protestant.

◆

St. Benedict's Rule, chapter 16: "'Seven times in the day,' says the Prophet [psalmist], 'I have rendered praise to you.' Now that sacred number of seven will be fulfilled by us if we perform the offices of our service at the time of the morning office, of prime, of terce, of sext, of none, of vespers and of compline, since it was of these day hours that he said, 'Seven times in the day I have rendered praise to you.' For as to the night office the same Prophet says, 'In the middle of the night I arose to glorify you.'"

It is important to remember that the hours of prayer we find here were designed by monks for monks and for a monkish life. It is not often possible for a layperson to rise at midnight, haul one's body to a church, and pray vigils with the church, and neither is it convenient to interrupt the work schedule in the morning for terce or to stop whatever one is doing in the afternoon for none. It is, however, possible to find enough rhythm in the day for the ordinary person to pray two or three offices: lauds, sext, or vespers, and compline. "Possible," I say, but still difficult. Hence, for many laypersons who seek to pray with the Church according to the sacred rhythms of the Divine Office, the most practicable method is to pray morning prayer (lauds) and evening prayer (vespers).

What does one do in the "offices" of prayer at the various hours of prayer? One answer to this is to pray what is called *The Liturgy of the Hours*. This four-volume set of prayers is the official modern Roman Catholic version of the kind of prayer established by St. Benedict for his communities of faith. Something like this has been prayed for centuries by the women and men in the monastic tradition. And, for the many laity who have ventured into such a commitment, it has been prayed outside the monastic tradition. Sometimes this prayer book is called *The Breviary*. There is a one-volume edition called *Christian Prayer*. There are other, less-than-official versions, but whichever one you find, you will be holding in your hands the essence of the Benedictine prayer tradition.

And here we come to a roadblock for many Protestants: The Church is split in three major ways—Orthodoxy, Catholicism, and Protestantism. If you imagine with me that you are walking from your *Portiuncola* into the basilica, you will see that the Church is neatly divided into three groups. The prayer books of each tradition both resemble and differ from the others. "Why," I have been asked more than a few times when I have suggested to Protestants that they use *The Liturgy of the Hours*, "should we use the prayer books of the Catholics or the Orthodox?" My answer is always the same: Most of the prayer book is the Psalms (which are from the Bible, a good Protestant answer), and the prayers are good prayers. Much of what we find in the prayer books was established well before there was any such thing as what we now know to be the Eastern Orthodox Church or the Roman Catholic Church. Some of what we find, of course, transgresses typical Protestant strictures. Protestants may have a problem with how often Mary shows up in some of these prayers. What Protestants need to wrestle with is that Mary herself prophesied that she would be called "blessed" by all future generations. When we find Mary in the prayer book, we Protestants will be challenged to give thanks to God for the most important woman in church history: the mother of Jesus.

The four-volume *The Liturgy of the Hours* is far and away the most complete prayer book in the history of the Church, and it is to everyone's advantage to know what it contains.

It takes some getting used to, but it is worth the effort. Kris and I were both reared in non-liturgical traditions, so much of the language of liturgy has been an acquired taste. For instance, at one point Kris thought "vespers" meant prayers, so she began calling Morning Prayers "morning vespers." This name has stuck with us, so we pray both morning vespers and evening vespers! (Benedict, I hope, would enjoy the nonsense of the expression.)

Now, back to the prayer book of the Roman tradition.

THE LITURGY OF THE HOURS

The most *complete* prayer book in the history of the church, whether one looks to the Eastern Orthodox, the Roman Catholic, or the Anglican and other Protestant communions, is the Roman Catholic *The Liturgy of the Hours*. However, it is also the most *complex* prayer book, a factor that deters some from using it. Some have tried to use it and given up, but there are others who have figured it out, and their number is growing. I can vouch for its complexity, but I have figured it out—I think.

On a flight from Chicago to Minneapolis, I sat next to a young woman who looked tired. As she sat down, she quieted herself and seemed to be praying. Then she pulled out a green book filled with ribbons and small bookmarks, stuff hanging out and other things falling out. (Anyone who knows someone who uses *The Liturgy of Hours* knows whereof I speak!) I recognized her green book as a volume of *The Liturgy of the Hours* for Ordinary Time (roughly from

Pentecost to Advent). Knowing that it is complicated to use, I asked her to explain it to me. She tried, bless her heart, but there wasn't enough time to make everything clear. "Start with the Invitatory," she said, "and then go here and then there." I was lost. What's an "Invitatory," I asked myself? Eventually, because I was determined to use *The Liturgy of the Hours*, I figured it out, so let me say a few words.

First, there are several editions and variant names, and some of the editions are official and some are not. I suggest getting a copy of *The Liturgy of the Hours* or a shortened version and taking the plunge. A day ordered by the Divine Office sanctifies the heart and draws us into the basilica to pray with the Church.

◆

"Think of the recent media coverage of faithful Muslims who stop four [five] times a day—at work, at home, while traveling—and pray toward Mecca. This is a countercultural practice: To stop commerce, travel, conversation, even ministry (!). To stop for a short time the advancement of an individual, and by extension society, in order to make an offering to God. Our culture does not reward those of us who stop three or four times per day . . . but God does. God rewards the one who practices the Office with peace and with an intimacy of relationship that truly is the meaning of life." —TONY JONES

Second, there are seven hours of prayer currently in use, and *The Liturgy of the Hours* takes those committed to praying with the Church in this manner through each of them. For instance, following the directions from *The Liturgy of the Hours* for Morning Prayer (lauds) just this morning I prayed the Invitatory ("Lord, open my lips. And my mouth will proclaim your praise") and Psalm 95 (which is prayed every morning) and then moved to Week I, Monday morning prayer, and said (not sang) a hymn (I imagined Benedictine voices), most of Psalm 5, and a short prayer about that psalm. Then I was invited to pray 1 Chronicles 29:10–13, Psalm 29, and another short prayer. Next I was directed to recite 2 Thessalonians 3:10–13, say a short responsory prayer, then (as for each morning) the Canticle of Zechariah from Luke 1. The morning session ended, as it does each day, with some intercessions, the Lord's Prayer ("Our Father"), and then two concluding prayers.

Morning prayer took about fifteen minutes, and I said everything aloud. This may look confusing, but it is not hard to follow in the book because it is laid out for you. There are shorter sessions for midmorning, midday, and midafternoon, then a lengthier evening prayer before finishing off with night prayer. For the brave of heart, the day begins at midnight, with the office of readings.

Third, each office of the day has its own focus. The office of readings (vigils) focuses on reading designated sacred texts (such as a text from St. Augustine), and compline (night prayer) focuses on confession and praying for health. Fourth, the heart of it all is the Psalms, and one who follows the entire *Liturgy of the Hours* will recite the entire Psalter each month—that's right, all 150 psalms every month.

Finally, let me suggest that you get help if you want to learn how to use *The Liturgy of the Hours*. Perhaps the easiest guide I have found is by Madeline Pecora Nugent, a happy and humorous housewife who has prayed each of the seven hours for years. Her book is called *The Divine Hours for Dodos (Devout, Obedient Disciples of Our Savior)*—and she'll make feeling like a dodo fun.

Let me be honest. It takes commitment to learn how to pray with the Church using *The Liturgy of the Hours*, and the reason is simple: Much of what you are to do is not in the book (you're expected to know it, dodo) and there is so much moving from one part of the book to another that you may feel distracted (you're expected to have lots of it memorized, dodo).

NOT JUST FOR MONASTICS

Though it takes work to learn *The Liturgy of the Hours*, the use of morning prayer and evening prayer (and night prayer) is within the reach of anyone with a commitment to pray with the Church. And I have found the structured order of the tradition to be both worshipful and joyous.

One of my favorite fiction writers, Flannery O'Connor, who tragically died at thirty-nine from lupus, was a devout Catholic in what she called the "Christ-haunted South." A recent book about her by Ralph Wood says this of her sacred rhythms of prayer:

Her days began with early mass when it was available and she was mobile. Even after she was largely confined to the farmhouse outside her rural Georgia home, O'Connor often attended the service of Benediction of the Blessed Sacrament at her parish church. Her days ended with prayers from her bedside missal, as she made her confessions and petitions in consort with the church universal.

She also made it a habit to read from St. Thomas Aquinas every night before bed for twenty minutes—an adaptation of the office of readings. O'Connor herself, in her book *The Habit of Being*, said this of her prayer practices: "I say Prime in the morning and sometimes I say Compline at night." While studying at the prestigious writing school at the University of Iowa, where she established her career as a writer, O'Connor attended services at St. Mary's "practically every morning . . . [and] as soon as I went in the [church] door I was home." She prayed, as it were, both in her own *Portiuncola* and in the basilica *with* the church.

Thomas Merton, who was active during the lifetime of Flannery O'Connor, said this of her upon her untimely death: "When I read Flannery O'Connor, I do not think of Hemingway, or Katherine Anne Porter, or Sartre, but rather of someone like Sophocles. What more can you say of a writer?" O'Connor's single-minded focus to unlock the mysteries of human nature, made so visible and graphic in her grotesque imagery, was in no small measure the result of her prayer life—a life of praying with the Church according to the rhythms of the Divine Office.

There is no reason that I can see (nor spiritual merit) in limiting oneself to only one of the major prayer books, for each of them offers to the whole Church what it means to pray with the Church. Henri Nouwen, a Catholic priest, showed flexibility in his own prayer life because he drew upon the Eastern Orthodox tradition by regularly reciting the Jesus Prayer. "Maybe," he said, "this is what makes the Jesus Prayer so good for me. Simply saying, 'Lord Jesus Christ, have mercy on me' a hundred times, a thousand times, ten thousand times, as the Russian peasant did, might slowly clean my mind and give God a little chance." But, as his biographer says, Nouwen "tried to foster the Liturgy of the Hours, the Jesus Prayer, and community meals wherever he happened to be. If guests visited him, they were always invited to join him for prayer at the appointed hour."

◆

Once when with Mother Teresa, Nouwen began to share all his wounds. Mother Teresa, in her inimitable way, offered a riposte: "Well, when you spend one hour a day adoring your Lord and never do anything which you know is wrong . . . you will be fine!" From this point on, for the rest of his life, Nouwen devoted an hour a day to prayer—largely connected to The Liturgy of the Hours.

—MICHAEL O'LAUGHLIN

His biographer says Nouwen was a "Dutchman who flew with God's angels."

OTHER PRAYER BOOKS

The Roman Catholic tradition is steeped in prayer, and it is not limited to prayer books. One thinks of the many who pray their way through a rosary. The beads are a physical, simple way of keeping track of where you are in a prayer of devotion. Another prayer tradition is the stations of the cross during Lent, where the faithful retrace the steps of Jesus to the cross on the *Via Dolorosa* ("the way of sorrows"). This practice is at least as old as the fourth century, and need not be limited to Holy Week. On each Friday in Rome there are fourteen stations placed around the Coliseum, and a Franciscan friar leads pilgrims in the prayers. (On Good Friday the Pope joins them.)

However, since this book is concerned with developing sacred rhythms with set prayers as a form of praying *with* the Church, I will turn back to Roman Catholic prayer books. Because *The Liturgy of the Hours* is somewhat cumbersome for travel, other prayer books have been developed in the Roman Catholic tradition, and I want to mention one of these that is being used throughout the world today—*The Glenstal Book of Prayer: A Benedictine Prayer Book*. For those who are contemplating the development of praying with the Church according to the hours of prayer in the Roman Catholic tradition, this is a good place to start.

This prayer book comes from the Benedictine community at Glenstal Abbey in Limerick, Ireland. The Benedictines there believe prayer is the "movement of the Holy Spirit in the human heart through which God reaches out and embraces human beings," and as ones who both sing the hours and long for more Christians to pray the hours with them, their "hope is that the duet sung by the Spirit and the human heart can expand into a cosmic hymn of praise to God, Creator, Redeemer, and Sanctifier of the world." Most important for beginners, everything is simplified to manageable proportions. There are morning and evening prayers, and "prayer stops" (terce, sext, none, compline), and then a gentle collection of other prayers Christians may find useful for a variety of reasons and seasons.

Though there are a variety of other simple prayer books such as *Benedictine Daily Prayer*, we are not surveying the entire prayer tradition but rather focusing on one or two examples as a form of inviting others to join us in the basilica to pray *with* the Church.

THE CONTRIBUTION OF THE MONKS

When I think of *The Liturgy of the Hours*, I think of what the monks have contributed to the prayer tradition of the church. In a sense, they drew upon everything from the days of Jesus onward and collected it all into a manageable prayer tradition.

What can we find there? Devotion to the praying of the Psalter, the recitation of the Lord's Prayer as Jesus taught us to pray, readings from the whole of Scripture, the transformation of prayer into a life of praise and adoration, the structuring of an entire life around the hours of prayer and the church calendar, the singing of Christian hymns, and the use of readings from outside the Bible to anchor the believer's life on the history of the Church. In other words, everything needful is here.

◆

From Hebridean Altars in Celtic Daily Prayer *(Meditations, Day 21):*

Seven times a day, as I work upon this hungry farm, I say to Thee, "Lord, why am I here? What is there here to stir my gifts to growth? What great thing can I do for others—I who am captive to this dreary toil?"

And seven times a day Thou answerest, "I cannot do without thee. Once did My Son live thy life, and by His faithfulness did show My mind, My kindness, and My truth to me. But now He is come to My side, and thou must take His place."

My own evangelical tradition emphasizes reading the Bible every day, focusing on daily (and especially) spontaneous prayers (sometimes morning and evening), and the use of both Psalms and Proverbs. In addition, I was always encouraged to read spiritual classics, though the ones we chose from the church tradition varied (apart from Augustine, who did not get the "St." before his name with us). Still, the elements of a fully developed sacred rhythm of prayer even for the Protestant tradition can be found in any of the prayer books.

And from each tradition you will surely find a prayer that perfectly expresses what your heart wants to say to God. I love to say night prayers (compline) *with* the Church. But, before ending with that office's closing prayer, I want to give a word of explanation. Among my favorite portions of Scripture are the first two chapters of the Gospel of Luke, wherein Luke records the glorious canticles of Zechariah, Mary, and Simeon. Every night *The Liturgy of the Hours* ends with the Canticle of Simeon, called the *Nunc dimittis*: "Now dismiss your servant in peace. . . ." Here Simeon readies himself to die because he has seen the Messiah. This passage is found in compline because the Church has always used the night prayer office to ponder the time when each of us will face death. Something like this is also found both in the Orthodox prayer book and in the Anglican *The Book of Common Prayer*. Here is the night prayer from *The Liturgy of the Hours*:

May the all-powerful Lord grant us a restful night and a peaceful death. Amen.

9

HOW THE ANGLICANS PRAY
WITH THE CHURCH

Christians all over the world quietly and gently begin the day and close the same day with *The Book of Common Prayer*. This prayer book derives from the efforts of the first Protestant Archbishop of Canterbury, Thomas Cranmer. (I trust the Anglicans will forgive Kris and me if we insist on calling him "Cremer." That "n" and "m" combo is not an easy one.) He gave birth to new church services and an orderly way of praying and reading the Bible that is now called *The Book of Common Prayer*, often abbreviated as *BCP*. Cranmer taught the English what to say when they gathered together to pray with the Church.

My wife's great-grandmother Burgess was one of those taught to pray using the *BCP*. In our possession now is a copy of her *Diary 1941*, from the days when she, an Episcopal Christian, lived as a widow in Lakeland, Florida, with her Lutheran sister-in-law, Caroline. Kris's great-grandmother attended Sunday morning and evening services, and apparently any others the local Episcopal parish offered. Her daily devotions were from the evening prayers of *The Book of Common Prayer*, but Caroline's preference was a Lutheran devotional called *The Day's Worship*.

On September 28, 1941, Great-grandmother Burgess closed her day with this record: "Read some, listened to the radio, had a light supper, and after devotions, am going to bed." On October 19 she was with her friend Caroline. "Caroline read the devotions . . ." and on November 29 she says, "Played our usual games of rummy, had devotions as usual, and went to bed." She passed the Episcopal faith on to her daughter, Mabel (Kris's grandmother). We have in our possession Mabel's copy of *The Book of Common Prayer*, a leather-bound gilt-edged slender volume that we have used off and on for several years. Her mother and her friend Caroline used an older version.

The *BCP* has gone through several revisions, and each modernization convulses many within the Anglican Communion. Recently an Episcopal priest told me he considered the 1979 version of the *BCP* a heretical version, while others welcome the changes as a breath of fresh air. Why? Because prayer books express the personal faith of those who become attached to them. A prayer book is a best friend—and only a few persons in the whole world can qualify as a best friend. Prayer books are like that: They are intimate companions for our journey. Prayer books are deeply personal because prayer itself is deeply personal.

Even as personal expressions of a tradition, each of the prayer books, not the least of which is *The Book of Common Prayer*, is rooted deeply in the sacred rhythms and tradition of Jesus so that each of them leads along the same path of praying *with* the Church. Each focuses on the Psalms, on the Scriptures, and on the Lord's Prayer. In addition to these integral elements the prayer books bring to expression the praise and hopes and theological emphases and internal intimacies of a church's tradition.

PRAYER BOOKS RECORD THE INTIMACY OF A FAITH TRADITION

When I was a little boy, my parents taught me to kneel next to my bed before going to sleep to pray the well-known prayer "Now I lay me down to sleep. . . ." One night when I was praying and my mother was (unknown to me) at the doorway watching to make sure I was saying my prayers, she said to me, "I can't hear you." To which I uttered (no kidding) what must have been said by many others, "I'm not talking to you." (Let me hasten to add that I doubt very much I was going heart to heart with God about something deeply personal—instead, I was probably in a hurry and tired, and in no mood to be interrupted.) It may have been that I was in the habit of daydreaming about a baseball player and that my mother was making sure I was sticking to the task, but what I said is true of genuine prayer. In prayer, we talk to God. We tell God what is on our hearts. No one else needs to hear us, not even Mom.

Nothing is more intimate than prayer. In the last year, as I was regularly thinking about this book on prayer, I often broke my reverie when I was with pastors to ask about their prayer lives. The most frequent response I got was a look rather than a response. That look asked this pointed question:

"Who do you think you are to ask me about my prayer life?" I did my best not to be offensive, but even with my efforts to be tactful, some thought such questions were a little too invasive. Some were embarrassed by how little they pray, some by what they are actually praying for, and others were just a little confused about prayer itself. Why did they feel probing was invasive? Because prayer is intimate stuff.

Prayer books, like the Psalter, record the prayers of others. When we learn to pray *with* the Church, we are invited to do so by reciting the intimate words of others as our own prayers. We are being invited to pray *with* those others in their words. Because prayer books are the intimate prayers of others, they are also the intimate faith of others, and that means that each prayer tradition will reflect the beliefs, hopes, words, and theology of that tradition.

◆

John Winthrop, first governor of Massachusetts Bay Colony, attended a school in which sacred rhythms of the prayer book tradition from the Anglican tradition were established (even though his own Puritan tradition departed from the Anglican tradition in some ways): "John's day," his biographer tells us, "would have begun at 5:00 AM when he gathered in the chapel with the rest of the collegiate community for morning prayer and a homily . . . [then daily studies]. A free period was followed by supper, then a review of the day's lessons before evening prayers at eight." —FRANCIS J. BREMER

Speaking of "tradition," why do we use the word "Amen"? This word transliterates an Aramaic word that means "so be it" or "it is established" or "I agree." It was a word for public prayers, and "Amen" was said by those who heard the prayer and agreed with it. Originally the person who said the prayer did not need to say "Amen"—surely people agree with their own words! I was in a crowded bus a while back when someone said that she was glad the Boston Red Sox had won the World Series just because it meant someone different had won—to which another bus rider said, "Amen!" This was not a religious event and it wasn't a prayer, but it illustrates what the word means. "Amen" means "I agree with what has been said and it is for me, too."

So, the word "Amen" is especially appropriate when we are using written prayers, like those in the Psalter or in the *BCP*. But saying "Amen!" involves uttering a full-hearted agreement with what was said. When we use the prayers of others they may say things we don't necessarily agree with, and they will surely say things in ways we might not. To pray *with* the Church involves the challenge of joining in the intimacy of other Christians, some of whom have beliefs, hopes, words, and a theology that are unlike our own. To pray *with* the Church involves courage, but this kind of courage expands our own hearts.

To pray using services from *A Manual of Eastern Orthodox Prayers* for the morning or evening is to pray *with* the Orthodox as they pray with the Church; to pray using *The Liturgy of the Hours* is to pray *with* the Roman Catholics as they pray with the Church; and to pray using *The Book of*

Common Prayer is to pray with the Protestants, the third major branch of the Christian church, as they pray with the Church. We are being asked not only to say in our creed that we believe in the communion of the saints but to say "Amen!" to it in a particular prayer. Each of these branches of the Church has its own prayer books, but each of these is rooted in the sacred rhythms and tradition established by Jesus. In each we will find some psalms and the Lord's Prayer and some Scripture readings, and in each we will also find distinctive contributions. The *BCP* contains both the sacred tradition of Jesus and its own prayers.

◆

My father gave me his little BCP for Morning and Evening Prayer. It includes the Scripture for each year, organized by day, with the rites right there. Except mine are leather bound, onion-skin paper, little dudes. . . . I pray Compline each night, and read the texts for the day. It is short, simple, and since the book is over my bed, very hard to forget. For me that helps a lot. —NATE

These big branches of the Church may never agree on theology (there are few signs of major breakthroughs here), but we can learn to pray *with* one another. We connect with one another with our hearts more easily than with our heads. As was mentioned earlier in this book, the Anglicans have a motto in Latin: *lex orandi, lex credendi,* meaning, "as we pray, so we believe." That is, they believe that though they may not agree on all matters of doctrine, they can at least worship and pray together, and by praying and worshiping together they can live together in peace.

But not all find this a welcoming challenge.

Some Christians break into hives when they hold the prayer book from another tradition. Some Anglicans don't care for *The Liturgy of the Hours*, and some Roman Catholics don't use the *BCP*, and some Orthodox don't use either of these. Those who were reared as I was in a tradition without prayer books, and who were taught that only spontaneous prayer is legitimate, sometimes develop a tic if it is suggested that we use any prayer book!

I remember the first time I held "Cremer" in my hands at St. Peter's Church, Toton, England. John Corrie, the curate, was reading. The copy in my hand was a clothbound, red, handsome *BCP*. I liked its feel in my hand, but I was lost in the service and needed some guidance. Everyone present seemed to know where to find what to say and when to say it, and it all went too fast for me to ask those around us what to say next. When we were singing a hymn I finally found it at about the second verse, but by now I was in no mood to sing it. But that was now inevitable, because there was no music in the hymn section of the *BCP Hymnal*. (I learned that the English label hymns with tunes and that they know tunes by a name—another hard thing that I still haven't learned, but there are musical reasons, or non-musical reasons, for that.)

We all feel this way when we encounter the prayer book of another tradition. Have you ever looked at the names of saints in the Orthodox prayer books? Who in the world is Moses the Hungarian? Or why does *The Liturgy of the Hours* have so many sections, and what are the "Proper of Seasons" and "Ordinary Time"? Why do the Anglicans call prayers "Collects"? Why do we feel so out of place when we pick up the prayer book of another church tradition? Because a prayer book embodies the intimate faith of a particular branch of the Church. Praying *with* other prayer books is sacred voyeurism (if there is such a thing). There is no faster way to the heart of another tradition in the Church than through its prayer book.

◆

David Adam, author of The Rhythm of Life: Celtic Daily Prayer, *spoke with Arthur Paul Boers about the growing interest in the prayers of sacred rhythms when Boers visited Adam's Anglican church, St. Mary Virgin, on the island of Lindisfarne on the North Sea:*

"Adam told me that since beginning his Holy Isle ministry, he's seen a 'great searching in people.' Many want guidance on prayer. He meets as many visitors as possible and offers counsel, support, and advice. He encourages people to pray at the same time as the services at St. Mary's, 'so that they feel they've got a link.'"

Like *A Manual of Eastern Orthodox Prayers* and *The Liturgy of the Hours*, the Anglican *Book of Common Prayer* expresses the heart of the faith of a particular branch of the Church.

Because Protestantism has varieties within itself, the *BCP* doesn't speak for the whole, but the distinctive beliefs of the Protestant faith can be found in the prayer book promoted by Thomas Cranmer. Cranmer taught England how to pray *with* the Church, and we too can learn to pray with the Church by praying with *The Book of Common Prayer*.

THE *BCP* REVITALIZED
BIBLE READING

It is hard for us today to imagine Christian living without thinking about some kind of Bible reading, but such was not the case for the first fifteen centuries of the Church. Most folks in the sixteenth century did not own a Bible or a prayer book. What people knew about the Bible they got from words spoken at church services. The protesters of the Reformation were convinced of a major need: The Church must get back to the Bible. So, to bring Christians back to the Bible, one of Cranmer's goals in life was to institutionalize in every church in England the practice of reading the Bible aloud according to a schedule that provided for the whole Bible to be heard each year. Each day the church bells would ring (at morning and evening), the locals would gather at the service, and they would begin to learn the Bible.

"In our public worship, in whatever tradition, we need to make sure the reading of Scripture takes a central place. In my own tradition," says

New Testament scholar N. T. Wright, "that of the Anglican Communion, the regular offices of Morning and Evening Prayer are, in all kinds of ways, 'showcases for scripture.' That is, they do with scripture (by use of prayer, music, and response) what a well-organized exhibition does with a great work of art: They prepare us for it, they enable us to appreciate it fully, and they give us an opportunity to meditate further on it."

Of course, the prayer books and church service books in use at the time of Cranmer recited portions of the Bible, but the leaders of the Reformation were persuaded that they didn't cover enough of the Bible. So Cranmer, in his holy discontent, designed a prayer book that did two things: It provided daily written prayers, and it provided daily readings from the Bible. To do this, Cranmer wove into the daily "offices," readings (called "Lessons") from the whole Bible. His most recent and very thorough biographer, Diarmaid MacCulloch, explains what the Archbishop did:

Besides setting out the new service orders, everything necessary to support the scheme [for Bible reading] was provided for: a table or kalendar [as he called it] of Bible readings designed to present the 'thread and order of holy Scripture' as far as possible in sequence 'entire and unbroken' through the year, and also a plan for reciting all 150 psalms each calendar month.

If there is any single theme that characterized the Reformation it was this: *sola scriptura* (Scripture alone). Faith, it was argued, was to be established by *first* going to the Bible. The prayer book in use for ordinary Christians needed to reflect *sola scriptura*. Out of this conviction came *The Book of Common Prayer*.

In my judgment one of the great contributions of the *BCP* to the church is its revitalization of Bible reading among the laity. The *BCP* asks ordinary Christians either to read the Bible or to listen to the Bible being read *aloud*. Here is one of the most important secrets of using prayer books: By using them, we read the Bible aloud to hear what God is saying to us, and along with reading the Bible we recite the prayers of the Church. These two acts, reading the Bible aloud and reciting the prayers of the church with others, constitute what it means to pray *with* the Church.

To this end, Thomas Cranmer and the ongoing shapers of *The Book of Common Prayer* set out schedules for reading the Bible in a one- or two-year cycle. The older version of the *BCP* had this schedule in the very beginning, while the more recent (1979) version has it toward the end, where it is called "The Daily Office Lectionary."

◆

"Indeed," again quoting N. T. Wright, "what is done in the classic offices of Morning and Evening Prayer, by means of listening to one reading from each Testament, is to tell the entire story of the Old and New Testaments, glimpsing the broad landscape of the scriptural

narrative through the two tiny windows of short readings. . . .
Scripture forms God's people, warming their hearts as with the disciples
on the road to Emmaus, so that their eyes may then be opened to know
him in the breaking of bread."

LET'S BE FLEXIBLE

The scheme for reading the Bible in a year or more found in
the Common Lectionary used by various Protestant denominations has been helpful for millions of Christians over the
years. However, many don't like to be told each day what
to read from the Bible. They prefer to read what they want
to read or to read at their own pace. Because of this, the
principle of flexibility has always accompanied most prayer
books. Some prefer the system of the institutional: For
them, the issue is one of discipline and constancy. They
prefer the whole Church to be reading the same texts
throughout the year. Others disagree. They believe God's
Spirit leads them to read what God's Spirit leads them to
read. Wisdom teaches us that we need to be flexible—some
don't do well reading for any length of time early in the
morning (I look at about fifty such persons during each
semester in my 8:00 AM Jesus of Nazareth class!).

John Stott, the former Rector of All Soul's Church,
Langham Place, London, and a well-known Anglican priest,
speaker, and author, is obligated by vocational calling to the
BCP. But John Stott exercises the principle of flexibility for
his own Bible reading plan. His recent biographer, Timothy
Dudley-Smith, describes Stott's routine, a routine Stott only

reluctantly made public for fear that many would think it the "secret" to his success.

> Well, you [the interviewer] are taxing me! I listen to the World Service of the BBC from 5 to 5:30 every morning while I am shaving and showering. . . . I have a glass of orange juice and make myself a cup of coffee and then I have a quiet time, of I suppose about an hour, in Bible reading and prayer; then I move on to reading a book, another book, doing some more serious Bible study. . . .

Stott, who has become a model for countless Bible expositors and pastors, tells us that he uses Robert Murray McCheyne's Bible Reading Calendar from 1842, which sets out a schedule for reading the Old Testament once a year and the New Testament twice.

It needs to be emphasized, especially for those who are prone to being either judgmental on themselves or critical of others, that flexibility is an important feature for Bible reading and even for developing sacred rhythms. It is OK to get bored with sameness, and it is OK to change one's reading patterns, and it is OK to miss a day or two. The BCP's plan for reading the Bible is as good as any of them, and it was Cranmer who got the Church of England on a Bible reading plan.

MANAGING THE "OFFICE" OR HOURS OF PRAYER

Another significant contribution of *The Book of Common Prayer* was to focus more of the devotional day on only two times of prayer: morning and evening. Cranmer knew that Benedict's *Rule* with its rigorous use of seven offices a day did not the fit the schedule of the ordinary Christian (or even the parish priest). Nor in fact does today's *The Liturgy of the Hours*, with its division of the day into the seven hours of prayer. Most of us have to adjust the hours to our own schedule so we can create our own sacred rhythms, and therefore many of us ask the church to be flexible with us. A good rhythm, Cranmer thought, is a twice-a-day sacred rhythm, in the morning and at evening.

Many have found the morning and evening sacred rhythm of the *BCP* to be a source of constant strength for life, and among them was C. S. Lewis. The Lewis scholar and former professor at Wheaton College, Lyle Dorsett, sums up Lewis's own prayer life with this:

> He normally read daily from the Anglican *Book of Common Prayer*, steeping himself in the Psalms. In fact, following the book's pattern, he read the daily office, and he most likely read through all 150 Psalms each month. During the academic term he also went to morning prayer, or Dean's Prayers, at 8:00 AM at Magdalen College. There he heard more Scripture read in this brief service of worship, meditation, and prayer. As frequently as possible he also liked

to set aside time in the late afternoon, preferably around 5:00 PM, when he could read other parts of the Bible and pray. George Sayer, who offered Lewis hospitality annually so that [the] two of them could hike the mountains of Malvern together, told me that Lewis almost invariably followed this pattern: After a good day's hike and tea, he would ask for a Bible if he had left his at home. Then he would retire to the guest room and pace up and down for about an hour, praying through portions of Scripture, often the Psalms.

This focus on the morning and evening is, in fact, a stroke of genius for many of us. I find these two times amenable to prayer and reading, and find the concentration on these times in the *BCP* particularly instructive. The concluding prayers for morning and evening prayers are my favorite prayers in the *BCP*. Here is the collect for the renewal of life that can be used during morning prayers:

O God, the King eternal, whose light divides the day from the night and turns the shadow of death into the morning: Drive far from us all wrong desires, incline our hearts to keep your law, and guide our feet into the way of peace; that, having done your will with cheerfulness during the day, we may, when night comes, rejoice to give you thanks; through Jesus Christ our Lord. Amen.

Here's a standard evening prayer (from the compline service):

Guide us waking, O Lord, and guard us sleeping; that awake we may watch with Christ, and asleep rest in peace. Amen.

Before we finish off this chapter on learning to pray with Cranmer and the *BCP*, we need to give a brief glimpse of what is involved in a set routine with the *BCP*.

A DAY WITH THE *BCP*

I have three editions of the *BCP* in my library: Grandma Mabel's 1789 version, the 1928 version re-certified in 1945, and the 1979 version certified in 1990. I also have a link to *The Book of Common Prayer* on my Web site (www.jesuscreed.org), so I can simply click on it in the morning or evening should I choose to. At that same site is the form of the *BCP* used in England, which is not the same as the 1979 Episcopal version. Take your pick, I say to those who want to learn how this segment of the church prays with the Church. One can use the *BCP* in a variety of ways, but two ways are for daily Bible reading or for a more orderly time of worship.

To use *The Book of Common Prayer* for Bible reading, we begin with the Lectionary at the end. It contains a guide for daily Bible reading called the "Daily Office Lectionary," and it is structured to take us through the Bible in two years. I find my place in the Church calendar (for example, I am writing this on 21 Sept 2005), and I go to the week called Proper 20 for Wednesday and find these readings for today's reading of the Bible:

Psalm 119:97–120; 2 Kings 6:1–23; 1 Corinthians 5:9–6:8.
Evening prayer is Psalms 81 and 82 and Matthew 5:38–48.

Following this schedule in a disciplined manner permits me to read through the Bible over two years.

To use the *BCP* for a worship time, we simply locate the morning prayer section or the evening prayer section at the front of the book. This involves a time of confession and praise very much like that of *The Liturgy of the Hours*. Today's morning prayer, for instance, goes through an Invitatory (a summons to worship) and the psalms for the day, then some lessons from the Bible and some canticles (biblical songs), the Apostles' Creed, the Lord's Prayer, the collect for the day (a special prayer), some prayers for other things, a general thanksgiving, the Prayer of St. Chrysostom, the Amen, and the Benediction. Good stuff, always.

Many have also found the list of "Prayers and Thanksgiving" in the *BCP* to be of use both personally and pastorally. It contains prayers for typical occasions in life— such as prayers for our country, for social justice, for the care of young persons, for a birthday, and thanksgivings for a variety of blessings. I mentioned the prayer for enemies from *A Manual of Eastern Orthodox Prayers* in a previous chapter, and here I will give the *BCP* version of such a concern as an example of what we find in this prayer book:

O God, the Father of all, whose Son commanded us to love our enemies: Lead them and us from prejudice to truth; deliver them and us from hatred, cruelty, and revenge; and in your good time enable us all to stand reconciled before you; through Jesus Christ our Lord. Amen.

AGAIN, IT TAKES SOME TIME

Kris and I have over time used the *BCP*. However, unless one is using the online editions that put everything in front of you, it is like *The Liturgy of the Hours* in that it takes some time to master where one is and what to say next, and where you need to keep your ribbons and bookmarks. You will again feel a bit lost for a while. But, it doesn't take long to learn the rhythms of the *BCP*.

There are three things about the *BCP* I most enjoy. I begin with the second because I have already dealt with it: The *BCP* enables the user to read most of the Bible in two to three years. The first favorite feature is the collects, short prayers designed for a particular day or season in the church calendar.

Here is the collect for one of the Sundays before Advent (Proper 29 today):

Almighty and everlasting God, whose will it is to restore all things in your well-beloved Son, the King of kings and Lord of lords: Mercifully grant that the peoples of the earth, divided and enslaved by sin, may be freed and brought together under his most gracious rule; who lives and reigns with you and the Holy Spirit, one God, now and for ever. Amen.

That final little flourish in this collect, "who lives and reigns with you and the Holy Spirit, one God, now and forever" is a constant ending to the *BCP*'s collects. It focuses on Trinitarian theology and closes off the prayer elegantly (not that all prayers have to be elegant).

◆

Almighty God our heavenly Father, you declare your glory and show forth your handiwork in the heavens and in the earth: Deliver us in our various occupations from the service of self alone, that we may do the work you give us to do in truth and beauty and for the common good; for the sake of him who came among us as one who serves, your Son, Jesus Christ our Lord, who lives and reigns with you and the Holy Spirit, one God, for ever and ever. Amen. —THE BOOK OF COMMON PRAYER, "FOR VOCATION IN DAILY WORK"

My third favorite element of the *BCP* is the thanksgiving prayers for the saints, wherein the church expresses gratitude for those who have gone before us. And my favorite Holy Day prayer is the thanksgiving to God for the life and example of Joseph, who is all but forgotten for many Christians. In fact, he did not even make an appearance in the older version of the *BCP*. In the modern version, here is the prayer:

O God, who from the family of thy servant David raised up Joseph to be the guardian of your incarnate Son and the spouse of his virgin mother: Give us grace to imitate his uprightness of life and his obedience to your commands; through Jesus Christ our Lord, who lives and reigns with you and the Holy Spirit, one God, for ever and ever. Amen.

Our commitment to the communion of saints is a commitment to more than the saints who now walk the earth. We are in communion also with all those who have walked this journey before us. The *BCP* brings us into contact with Christians all over the globe. Though it takes some getting used to, the *BCP* is a source of devotion and a guide for us as we learn to pray with the Church and read the Bible at the same time.

We have now completed our trip through the three major prayer books. Learning to pray with each, even if it is but a week or two a year, can teach us to pray *with* the Church. Each has its own distinctive emphases and, because each is the intimate record of the prayers of a segment of the church, it invites us into the inner chambers of each tradition. The awkwardness we may feel upon entry can be relieved over time if we will spend time with each so as to get to know our brothers and sisters in the faith.

Whichever tradition we find ourselves in, however often we pray in our own *Portiuncola*, an important element of spiritual formation is to learn to pray out in the basilica *with* the Church. The prayer books from each of the Christian traditions are designed to lead us into the Church to pray with the Church—so the Church can be formed as an instrument of grace for the good of our world.

10

HOW *THE DIVINE HOURS* PRAYS WITH THE CHURCH

"*P*raying ought to be easier than this" makes its way onto the lips of each of us who tries to pray with the major prayer books of the Church. By far, the most common complaint is that one has to have five or six ribbons, a couple of bookmarks, and an accurate memory to become comfortable with *A Manual for Eastern Orthodox Prayers* and *The Liturgy of the Hours* and *The Book of Common Prayer*. I have learned that it takes some time to get used to finding the appropriate collect or the intended concluding prayer. Sometimes I have just found one and prayed that collect or prayer and said to myself, "What difference does it make? This one sounds good."

On top of this, there are many of us who genuinely want to pray *with* the Church and don't want to have to pray with *only one* branch of the church when we do so. When we pray *The Liturgy of the Hours*, we are led to pray with the Church by the Roman Catholic prayer tradition; when we pray *The Book of Common Prayer* we are ushered into the larger basilica by the Anglican Communion; and when we pray *Eastern Orthodox Prayers* we learn to pray with the Church in the Orthodox manner. To be sure, with each of these we are led to pray *with* the Church and not just *in* the church alone. But, some of us want to pray in the sacred tradition of each. Coming into each of the prayer traditions challenges us because it involves a time commitment and perhaps some frustration to learn to pray with various prayer books. Like moving to a new house in a different neighborhood in an unknown city, changing prayer books requires time for us to become accustomed to the new tradition.

Is there an easier way? Is there a prayer book that avoids the ribbons and simply puts it all on the same page so we can sit down and say our prayers? Is there a prayer book that brings together the best from each tradition? The good news is that there is a prayer book that seamlessly joins the prayer books of the past into one single prayer book so that one can genuinely pray with the *whole* Church without having to pray with only one branch.

A JOURNEY OF PRAYER

If you are on a trek to learn to pray *with* the Church and not just alone in the church, begin with Phyllis Tickle's *The Divine Hours*, learn the sacred rhythms of morning and evening prayers, and then expand your set prayers to *The Liturgy of the Hours* and *The Book of Common Prayer* and *A Manual of Eastern Orthodox Prayers* (or other prayer books).

It took a layperson with a stubborn streak of independence to compose a prayer book for all of us. Several moments in her life need to be laced together to see how she learned the art of praying set prayers at fixed times.

Phyllis Tickle discovered the sacred rhythm of fixed-hour praying through both rebellion and providence. (God's ways are mysterious to most of us.) Phyllis grew up in the mountains of Eastern Tennessee in the home of a Baptist mother who prayed every afternoon at 3:30 PM, and a Methodist professor father. To keep their battles to a minimum, they became Presbyterians. When Phyllis's mother took her off to Shorter College (in Rome, Georgia), the first two things Phyllis did was buy a pack of cigarettes and start attending the Episcopal church. Her motive was simple and superficial sophistication.

"To become a true sophisticate-at-large," Phyllis says, "more than smoking was required. I would also have to turn myself into an Episcopalian." She continues:

> One must understand just here that at seventeen I had not the vaguest concept of what being an Episcopalian meant, nor did I even know many of them. . . . But the ones I did know were very attractive to me. In fact, based on my limited census, all Episcopalians were very wealthy, handsomely turned out, delightfully witty, socially able . . . in short, very sophisticated.
>
> What I was carrying in my head, of course, was a cliché; but the utility of clichés is that they speak the shorthand of the most apparent.

Which meant she would be attending St. Paul's in Rome, Georgia, and which meant she would soon be introduced to three things: the rhythms of morning prayer on Sunday morning, the Psalter the Episcopalians read, and (most of all) *The Book of Common Prayer*. Her "conversion" to the Anglican communion took more than a decade, but by the time she and her physician husband, Sam, were settled near Memphis, Phyllis Tickle had come to terms with an important element in her life: the power of sacred rhythms, or what she calls fixed-hour prayer.

DISCOVERING THE MEANING OF AN ORDERED LIFE

But first she needed to learn the value of rhythms in life.

As a college student Phyllis suffered from depression but she made a discovery that helped her significantly. Phyllis sat down one day with a pencil and a sheet of paper to block off her week in seven columns. She then filled in each day with her study schedule. Upon completing it, she looked at it and saw a pattern—and this pattern in and of itself brought healing to her life. On Sunday, she did this . . . on Monday, she did that . . . etc. She saw an order to her life. This sense of order soon began to shape Phyllis's spiritual quest, for she became convinced that her prayer life would also need to be ordered.

College, however, does not often encourage an ordered prayer life.

But, in college, young students encounter the best minds in history, one of whom is René Descartes, the famous French polymath and, as the French might say, *gentilhomme*—gentleman sophisticate. In his studies Descartes found himself embarrassed at his colossal ignorance, but he also discovered that certainty was to be found in mathematics and science. Descartes created, almost single-handedly, the modern era's absolute devotion to the scientific basis of knowledge. So committed to the mind was Descartes that he came to the conviction that the one thing he was assured of was his own existence, and he knew he existed for this reason: "I think, therefore I am." That is, because I can reason, I exist.

Phyllis found her own existence elsewhere, and her findings reflect a depth of insight not often met in young college students: "With all due respect to Descartes' earlier solution, the truth for me at that moment [of discovering my life was patterned] was that if what I was had pattern, *then I was*." For Descartes, existence followed from thinking; for Phyllis Tickle, existence followed from living an ordered life.

The need for an ordered pattern to her life led her to produce a prayer book that resolved the problem of using multiple ribbons and switching pages and finding the right prayer. Meet *The Divine Hours*.

◆

I have recently started using The Divine Hours *by Phyllis Tickle, which lists the fixed-hour prayers for each day of the year. Not having grown up in that kind of tradition or even attending a church that practices it, I have absolutely LOVED it. I find praying fixed-hour prayers has helped me throughout the day to develop having the mind of Christ.* —MARK PERRY

PRAYING WITH *THE DIVINE HOURS*

In September of 2000, Phyllis Tickle's *The Divine Hours: Prayers for Autumn and Wintertime* appeared, and then this volume of prayers was followed by *Prayers for Springtime* and *Prayers for Summertime*: three volumes that are easier to use than a fork and constitute the most ecumenical prayer book I know of.

The Divine Hours is a good place to start for any person who wants to learn to pray *with* the Church. Each week of prayers in *The Divine Hours* begins with Sunday, and you merely have to find the Sunday closest to the date (today is Monday, December 12, and that puts one in the week beginning on a Sunday closest to 12 December). Find Monday, find morning prayers, and off you go. Put the ribbon in that spot, and you won't have to shuffle from one part of the prayer book to another to find where you are.

Each "divine hour" (which takes about 5–10 minutes) has a sacred rhythm:

The Call to Prayer (the same as the Invitatory of other prayer books)

The Request for Presence (invoking God's presence)

The Greeting (of God's presence)

The Refrain (like the antiphons of other prayer books)

A Reading (usually from the Gospels)

The Refrain

The Morning/Midday/Vespers Psalm (a selection of one psalm)

The Refrain

The Cry of the Church
The Lord's Prayer
The Prayer Appointed for the Week (a collect from the
BCP)
The Concluding Prayers of the Church (from a prayer
book)

Vespers, or evening prayer, and compline, or night
prayer, each have slight adjustments in accordance with the
prayer-book tradition. The compline readings include some
readings from spiritual classics and give one a sense of the
office of readings in *The Liturgy of the Hours*.

◆

In Arthur Paul Boers' book The Rhythm of God's Grace, *Arthur
tells of an interview he had with Phyllis Tickle, who was then the
Editor for Religion for* Publisher's Weekly. *She observed, says
Boers, that the surge of interest in prayer books shows that we are "rapidly hastening toward the third century."*

THESE PRAYERS ARE OURS

A few years ago I learned about *The Divine Hours* from a friend,
so I acquired the first volume, *Prayers for Autumn and Wintertime*.
Kris and I began to say morning prayers and evening prayers
together and have maintained the sacred rhythm ever since.
We don't try to get something special from them each time,
and we are not looking to learn something new on every

occasion, but instead we are doing what millions of Christians have done for two millennia: We are simply reciting the prayers of the Church, centered as they are around the Psalter and the Lord's Prayer, to remind ourselves of something old as we express our worship to God.

We do not pray with the Church and *The Divine Hours* until we get some ecstatic blessing. I find that the sacred rhythm centers my life, orders my day, enlarges my heart, reminds me of old truths, and provides me with words to express both what I feel and think as well as what is appropriate at this time of the year in the Church calendar. *The Divine Hours* has become our prayer book. When I pick up the book in the morning or evening, I often wander in my mind into the basilica and imagine joining up with Christians throughout the world.

In fact, I bought two copies of each volume so I could have one when I traveled and not deprive Kris of the sacred rhythm. I carry one in my book bag when I commute and travel, and I have found myself saying prayers in airports, hotel lobbies, and airplanes. Anywhere and at anytime, as Pilgrim and Benedict and Cranmer have taught us, are the places and the *time* for saying our prayers.

FRIENDLY, ECUMENICAL, AND COMPREHENSIVE

The Divine Hours is friendly. There are only three things to learn. First, that the standard set prayers of the church, the Gloria and the Lord's Prayer, are found on the facing page of each month. Here is one simple thing to do when you get *The Divine Hours*: Memorize the Gloria[+] and the Lord's Prayer. Second, you need only one ribbon: Place it in the next office you will be praying. That is, after morning prayer I place mine at evening prayer, since I rarely say midday prayer. Third, if you want to do compline before bedtime, the compline prayers are found at the end of each month—and they are given in a weekly routine. So, at compline you will find Sunday through Saturday prayers— when you get to Saturday, you go back to Sunday for the next night. (Some might toss in an extra bookmark at the compline prayers.)

Learning to pray *with* the Church is designed to be do-able, not something that takes hours. But, neither is it something that we should be able to pull off in thirty seconds or less. *The Divine Hours* will take about ten to fifteen minutes per office; the *BCP*, if one is reciting all the Scripture texts with it, could take fifteen to thirty; and *The Liturgy of the Hours* takes about ten to fifteen minutes for most offices. So, while it takes a firm commitment to stop twice (for morning and evening) or three times or four times (if one adds in midday and compline), the actual recitation time is manageable for even the busiest of Christians.

Not only is *The Divine Hours* accessible, it is also ecumenical—though it is a little shy on the Orthodox side. Phyllis Tickle, bless her heart (which I can say since she's Southern), has chosen the best prayers in the traditions of

[+] "Glory be to the Father, and to the Son, and to the Holy Spirit. As it was in the beginning, is now, and ever shall be, world without end. Alleluia. Amen."

both *The Liturgy of the Hours* and *The Book of Common Prayer.* There is a clear favoring of the collects of the *BCP* as the prayer for the week, not just because she is Episcopalian but also because these are among the best prayers in the history of the church for weekly prayers. I like to say I'm biased and accurate at the same time. But, with a proper introduction to the prayers of others we discover that we have prayer friends all around the world, in the Orthodox world, in the Roman Catholic world, and in the Protestant world.

◆

G. K. Chesterton, quoted in The Divine Hours, *said this:*

Once I found a friend

"Dear me," I said, "he was made for me."

But now I find more and more friends

Who seem to have been made for me

And more and yet more made for me,

Is it possible we were all made for each other

all over the world?

In addition, *The Divine Hours* is comprehensive. Not exhaustive, but comprehensive, it covers the whole day and the whole Church calendar. A complete prayer book would be too big to be useful if we expected it to give us the best prayers of the Church and all of the Psalter and all of the Bible and all of the best spiritual readings, all in a nice wor-shipful order for every office of the day. Not only that, it would be too expensive for ordinary people. So, *The Divine Hours* is a comprehensive introduction to prayers, to worship, to the psalms, and to classical hymns, with a sampling of all that is important. *The Divine Hours* is *iconic*: it leads the person praying into the Psalms, into the hymnal, into the Bible, and into prayers from throughout the history of the Church.

Finally, *The Divine Hours* is selective. Because the intent was to get everything into three affordable volumes, we are treated to selected verses from the Psalter and the rest of the Bible (from *The New Jerusalem Bible*), as well as selected prayers that have stood the test of time in the history of the Church. Each morning's prayers conclude with a dedicatory prayer of our lives to God that is drawn from the *BCP*. I pray this prayer every morning, and I have grown to appreciate it more and more.

Lord God, almighty and everlasting Father, you have brought me in safety to this new day: Preserve me with your mighty power, that I may not fall into sin, nor be overcome by adversity; and in all I do, direct me to the fulfilling of your purpose; through Jesus Christ our Lord. Amen. [When others join me, we pray "us" and "we" instead of "me" and "I."]

The classical prayer book from the Catholic tradition, *The Liturgy of the Hours*, uses three canticles from the first two chapters of Luke's Gospel every day: the *Benedictus* (Zechariah's song), the *Magnificat* (Mary's Song), and the *Nunc Dimittis* (Simeon's Song). The first is used at morning prayer, the second at evening prayer, and the third at night prayer. Because the adaptation of the *Nunc Dimittis* is so suitable for a prayer that one prays just before going to bed, I provide it here in the version that *The Divine Hours* provides for compline prayers:

> Lord, you now have set your servant free to go in peace as you have promised; for these eyes of mine have seen the Savior, whom you have prepared for all the world to see: a Light to enlighten the nations, and the glory of your people Israel.
>
> Glory to the Father, and to the Son, and to the Holy Spirit: as it was in the beginning, is now, and will be for ever. Amen.

NOT JUST FOR EPISCOPALIANS

Phyllis Tickle's *The Divine Hours* derives from the Anglican prayer tradition and favors the collects of *The Book of Common Prayer*, but folks from various traditions use these prayer books too. Recently Kris and I were in Ann Arbor, Michigan, and we heard that Phyllis was at the Ann Arbor Vineyard, a charismatic fellowship. Charismatic churches lean toward the spontaneous, so it was a surprise to us to learn that this local Vineyard fellowship was promoting the online publication and use of *The Divine Hours*.

We went to the Vineyard for the evening to a packed house. The service began with people standing, waving hands in praise, and dancing, and the band was rocking—

my memory was that the band was comprised of tattooed sorts and long-haired types and ordinary folks all mixed into one rocking band. The music was loud, the worship was expressive, and Phyllis was clapping and swaying with the best of them.

The pastor, Ken Wilson, stood up and said pointedly, "Phyllis Tickle taught me to pray." He then introduced Phyllis to the audience, and she sat atop a stool that was brought for her. She calmly observed that when you give an Episcopalian a stool, you should also give her a drink! Which they didn't, but they knew the sophisticated stereotype of which she spoke.

The Vineyard Fellowship of Ann Arbor illustrates a tendency in the church in North America. Many Christians are discovering the formative potency of fixed-hour prayers, of what I call sacred rhythms, and accompanying this discovery is a desire to connect with the church throughout the ages and across traditions. *The Divine Hours* is one of the most accessible endeavors in the history of the church to provide for ordinary Christians, from the various traditions, a manageable set of prayers that can become a gateway to the development of a consistent, meaningful, and rhythmical prayer life.

CONCLUSION

11

PRAYING WITH THE CHURCH:
FOLLOWING JESUS DAILY,
HOURLY, TODAY

e began this book with the image of St. Francis's *Portiuncola* inside the Basilica of St. Mary of the Angels. This image served us well in describing two kinds of prayer: personal, private devotion—praying *in* the church; and public, communal worship—praying *with* the church. We have focused our efforts in this book on praying *with* the Church rather than praying *alone inside* the church.

In this concluding chapter we want to look at the big picture at how we can, as individuals, adapt a practice of praying *with* the Church in our own context. Not everyone lives near a church that practices both morning and evening prayers, and so we have to be realistic: How can you and I learn to pray *with* the Church? There are a number of suggestions that we can offer, and I have chosen the following ones as we seek to develop sacred rhythms for spiritual formation.

◆

"In prayer we pay attention as the Holy Spirit breathes God's voice to us, and we breathe back our sighs and songs of love and praise. We call out to the heart of God and we listen to the word of God as it has been given through the centuries—words of Scripture, canticles, teachings, and devotional readings." —THE LITTLE BOOK OF HOURS

FIRST, WE NEED REALISTIC EXPECTATIONS

If you are like me, you might be tempted right now to get online and order each of these prayer books—or, if you are even more like me, by the time you have read this far, you may have already done this! But we have our own schedules and routines to live with, and it is nearly impossible for lay people to adapt a seven-offices-per-day sacred rhythm to our lives. So, let's start with a dose of reality: Avoid the heroic.

As Esther de Waal states in her classical study of Benedictine spirituality, we need to avoid thinking we can begin tomorrow praying each of the seven hours or committing ourselves to the all of the prayers and devotions of the entire *Book of Common Prayer*. As she puts it,

Before I try to impose upon myself any idealized "Christian life" or undertake any demanding (and probably guilt-inducing) spiritual marathon, I should look around me and see that seeking God does not demand the unusual, the spectacular, the heroic.

My suggestion for each of us (and one that I follow myself) is to begin with a minimal expectation: either a morning session or an evening session or, if it is realistic, both a morning and an evening session.

I also suggest diving first into the prayer book tradition closest to your own faith tradition—if you are Presbyterian, try *The Book of Common Prayer* before you delve into the prayer books of the Orthodox or the Roman Catholics. And, if you are Roman Catholic, start with *The Liturgy of the Hours* before attempting to use Phyllis Tickle's *Divine Hours*.

SECOND, WE NEED TO TRY

The best way to learn to pray *with* the Church is to get a prayer book, start saying prayers, and find a mentor to help you. I tell my students all the time that the best way to learn to write is twofold: Write often and read good writers. The best way to learn to pray with the Church is to simply start praying with the Church and reading prayers that have been written for the Church.

The easiest way to begin is with the most user-friendly prayer books—either *The Divine Hours* or the *Glenstal Book of Prayer*. If you are looking for another beginner's prayer book, try *The Little Book of Hours: Praying with the Community of Jesus*, which contains one month of morning, midday, and evening prayers, and a compact compline office as well. Perhaps you are committed to your own church tradition and its prayer book, and you are determined to use only that one. Then get one and ask someone to help you and give it a go (as they say in England). You can nearly always find someone to help you. Your pastor or priest can usually guide you here.

I would also suggest that once you've got the hang of a prayer book—say a year or so, because there is no reason to hurry and you've got a lifetime to learn—that you broaden your praying *with* the Church by sampling other prayer books. I have a number of prayer books, and I've used each: *The Book of Common Prayer, The Liturgy of the Hours, The Divine Hours, A Manual of Eastern Orthodox Prayers, Benedictine Daily Prayer, Celtic Daily Prayer,* and *The Glenstal Book of Prayer.* My standard prayer book is *The Divine Hours,* but each prayer book is of value to me in different seasons. In each of them we discover the basic elements of Jesus' sacred tradition, and we also find the distinct elements of different branches of the Church.

THIRD, WE NEED SPACE FOR SILENCE

People who pray *with* the Church, unless they have taken monastic vows and say their prayers in unison in a monastery chapel, will tell you this: They have a *space* where they find *silence* for prayer. A sacred space is a place where our own prayer life can become a living and vibrant reality.

Most of us need such a space for our prayers. For some it is no more than a window through which one can see a meadow or our back garden or a mountain or our neighborhood or a body of water or a hill. For some it might be slipping into the quiet of a chapel or a church or a cathedral. For others it may be a chair surrounded by clutter or kids' toys or books. When at home, I like to pray at the end of the couch; on days I teach, I pray in my yellow chair in my office; when I travel I often find a chair where I can recollect myself to say my prayers. Such sacred places and spaces become for us a spot where, as Margaret Silf says it so well, "the presence of the invisible and the spiritual . . . is almost palpable."

◆

Sacred space is perhaps most graphically seen in the famous Roussanou Monastery in the Meteora, Greece.* Here, where wind and time have carved out massive towers of rock that stand erect over the plains of Thessaly, one spots small communities atop mighty rock towers. To find a sacred space for prayer and devotion, the medieval monks ascended these towers of rock to build monasteries, the most famous of which is the Roussanou Monastery. It is accessible only by a narrow bridge from another crag.

Somehow we are able in that sacred space to regain what the 131st psalm describes. This is perhaps the only psalm written by a woman, and I quote it from the sixteenth-century Coverdale translation found in *The Book of Common Prayer*:

---

* Photos can be seen at http://www.photoseek.com/greece/Meteora.html.

Lord, I am not high-minded; I have no proud looks.
I do not exercise myself in great matters which are too high for me.
But I *refrain my soul,* and keep it low, like as a child that is weaned from his mother: yea, my soul is even as a weaned child.

The wording, perhaps because it is so odd for us, stops us in our tracks: What does *"refrain* my soul" mean? The NRSV has "calmed and quieted," and that is surely the sense. To "refrain" means to hold in check, to calm down, to find a place of quietude within. The psalmist continues this line of thinking: As a child is sated after breastfeeding, so we are to quiet ourselves to God.

All prayer requires us to become quiet, and most people find a place that connects them to this quietude. It is also a place of silence—not in the sense of the absence of noise but in the sense of attentiveness to God. Ruth Haley Barton uses a potent image in describing what this place of silence is like. Her spiritual director, when she realized how disjointed Ruth's life really was, said this to her: "Ruth, you are like a jar of river water all shaken up. What you need is to sit still long enough that the sediment can settle and the water become clear." And that is what a sacred space of silence is: It is simply a place where the distractive sediments of our own life can settle long enough for us to see who we are so we can come to God in utter honesty. Gravity can do its own work if we let it. Silent spaces are not, as Ruth states, "self-indulgent exercises for times when an overcrowded soul needs a little time to itself. Rather, they are concrete ways of opening to the presence of God beyond human effort and beyond the human constructs that cannot fully contain the Divine."

What praying *with* the Church teaches us is that we are invited into this quiet, sometimes alone and sometimes with others in the basilica. Solitude is found only by attentiveness, and attentiveness can be discovered both in the *Portiuncola* and in the basilica.

FOURTH, WE NEED VARIETY AND FLEXIBILITY

Nothing is more damaging to vital prayer than dull and vain repetition. For this reason alone, praying with the Church involves both variety and flexibility. Because they contain so little variety, I could not pray the Eastern Orthodox morning and evening prayers day in and day out. But, I pick them up occasionally. The *Glenstal Prayer Book* has only one week of prayers, and after praying them for a while I begin to itch for a little variety.

Anyone who prays *with* the Church very long knows that the Church has always encouraged both variety and flexibility. Here are two good examples: *The Liturgy of the Hours* runs to four volumes, revolves around the Psalter, but has enough variety in its office of readings to stimulate the soul for an entire year—and by the time one finishes, one is ready to start all over again. Its fullness offers a lifetime of prayers. And *The Book of Common Prayer* encourages persons to use a variety of prayers along with reading through the whole Bible.

The Psalter itself contains prayers that encompass the whole of human experience—from prayers of confession to praise, from complaints and moans and doubts to screaming prayers for vindication and justice, from quiet reflections to long songs of thanksgiving for the Torah. Its different prayers stimulate each of us differently at different times. We need each of these types of prayer over the course of a lifetime.

Spending time in the major prayer books of the Church, and joining in prayer with other Christian traditions as those Christians stand in the basilica to pray with the Church, can provide a boost to our prayer life.

We need not limit ourselves to one prayer-book tradition. We might dedicate the summer to *The Book of Common Prayer*, and the autumn to *The Liturgy of the Hours*, and the winter season to something else. If we find ourselves comfortable with one, we can stick with it, but we may become sensitive enough to our own soul to realize we are getting stuck and that we want to keep praying with the Church but in a different spot in the basilica. Retreats are held all over the world, and we could take a weekend to go on a retreat to learn, for example, how to use the *Benedictine Daily Prayer* book. Sometimes we try new restaurants, and sometimes we can try new prayer books. See how they work, listen to their rhythms, learn to pray with a different branch of the Church.

I was recently struck by hymns found in the Roman Catholic The Liturgy of the Hours. *For a morning prayer the worshiper is asked to sing "Breathe on Me, Breath of God," by Edwin Hatch, an Anglican pietist, and we are invited in an evening prayer to sing the famous hymn "Amazing Grace," written by the Anglican John Newton.*

So, yes, we need to permit ourselves both variety and flexibility. But variety and flexibility need to rotate around a disciplined core of practices. So, let us say that you are using *The Divine Hours* and find your prayer becoming dull: Stop for a week, pick up a prayer book from a different tradition, and practice that for a week. Then return to *The Divine Hours*. Or, vary your use of *The Divine Hours*. For example, instead of reading the day's selected portion of Scripture, find that passage of Scripture and read the whole passage—either from the Psalter or the Gospels. Variety needs to depend on something stable from which it varies.

Prayer, like love, seeks intimacy through variety in constancy.

Here's the only rule: Avoid making rules about prayer.

FIFTH, WE NEED DEPTH
AND BREADTH

To gain depth from the prayer-book traditions of the church we need to give ourselves at least one deep bath in a prayer book. This takes time—three months to a year. By using a prayer book over and over, we can absorb its ways of praise and worship and prayer. No one becomes an expert on the Jesus Prayer the first week, but those who have used the Jesus Prayer as a core practice throughout the day for months or years can tell you that it begins to anchor itself into the very fabric of our being.

The counting approach to prayers—whether it be the Jesus Prayer, the Rosary, or the Jesus Creed—misses the point. But, as one who says the Jesus Creed numerous times a day, when I am asked, "How many times today?" I can now say, "I'm not sure, but it has been with me all day long." Those who have learned to pray with the Church know whereof I speak: Time spent with prayers for the whole Church permits us to turn our lives into the Celtic infinite knot. The Celtic knot is a design of a rope that seemingly has no beginning or end, and is instead a symmetrical inter-twining that seems to go on and on forever. This image is exactly the sort of depth I am talking about when I speak of learning to pray with the Church. Over time, the prayers become us or we become the prayers or, better yet, both these things are true. In fact, we become the Church at prayer, even if we are in our own *Portiuncola*.

SIXTH, WE NEED TO KNOW
WHAT TO SAY FIRST:
ADORATION AND DEDICATION

Each of the prayer books has a similar beginning: The first words we utter are dedicatory and invitatory words, and in many traditions these words are prefaced by the sign of the cross. That is, they are words that express our openness to God, and they invite God into our space. This is a good practice: We gain our silence, and then we open our mouth to say something like this:

Lord, open my lips.
And my mouth shall proclaim your praise (*The Liturgy of the Hours*)

At this point, under the guidance of St. Benedict, the Christian recites the 95th psalm:

O come, let us sing to the LORD;
let us make a joyful noise to the rock of our salvation!
Let us come into his presence with thanksgiving;
let us make a joyful noise to him with songs of praise!
For the LORD is a great God,
and a great King above all gods.
In his hand are the depths of the earth;
the heights of the mountains are his also.
The sea is his, for he made it,
and the dry land, which his hands have formed.

O come, let us worship and bow down,
let us kneel before the LORD, our Maker!
For he is our God,
and we are the people of his pasture,
and the sheep of his hand. . . .

Then the Roman Catholic tradition recites *The Gloria* ("Glory be . . ."), which it attaches to all recitations of the psalms.

Most prayer traditions adapt this ancient structure of praise and adoration as the morning sun breaks. Both the Orthodox and the Anglican traditions dive first into confession before Psalm 95 is said. *The Divine Hours* varies the invitatory element every morning. Regardless, it has proven beneficial to many to begin the day with a prayer that invites God into our life and then dedicates one's life to God. Some use the famous prayer of St. Francis, which begins with "Lord, make me an instrument of your peace. . . ."

◆

A CELTIC PRAYER
WHEN DRESSING

I am giving Thee worship with my whole life,
I am giving Thee assent with my whole power,
I am giving Thee praise with my whole tongue,
I am giving Thee honour with my whole utterance.

I am giving Thee love with my whole devotion,

I am giving Thee kneeling with my whole desire,

I am giving Thee love with my whole heart,

I am giving Thee affection with my whole sense,

I am giving Thee my existence with my whole mind,

I am giving Thee my soul, O God of all gods.

SEVENTH, WE NEED TO USE THE PSALTER

If the Psalter was good enough to be Jesus' prayer book, it is good enough for ours. The Psalter is the prayer book of the Bible. There is no other. The Psalter is responsible for creating the prayers in the church. It remains the core of all Christian prayers.

Whenever we pray with psalms, we are joining the universal Church in prayer.

There are three ways I know of to make the Psalter our own. We can read the psalms (five a day) monthly in our own Bible. Or we can carry around a copy of *The Book of Common Prayer* so we can turn to it for daily reading of the Psalter; the advantage here is that the *BCP* has the Psalter divided into morning and evening readings for thirty days. And finally, we can rely on the reading schedule of a prayer book, such as *The Liturgy of the Hours*. This is fine if we pray each of the offices, but if we don't, we may want to take time to read the psalms that were used in the offices we didn't pray in their entirety.

However we read the Psalter, the minute we leave our own *Portiuncola* the first words we hear will be from the Psalter.

EIGHTH, WE NEED TO RECITE THE LORD'S PRAYER AND THE JESUS CREED EVERY DAY

Every prayer book makes use of the Lord's Prayer, or the Our Father, as one of its constant prayers. After all, Jesus taught us to pray the Lord's Prayer every time we pray (Luke 11:2: "when[ever] you pray, say: . . ."). Each of the prayer traditions incorporates the Lord's Prayer into every office.

When it comes to the Lord's Prayer, it is customary for some church traditions to finish it off with a closing benediction: "For thine is the kingdom, the power, and the glory, forever and ever. Amen." While these words were not said by Jesus according to the best and earliest manuscripts, many Christians say them because they consider it abrupt to finish with these words, "but deliver us from evil," and these closing words are based on an ancient Scripture, 1 Chronicles 29:11.

You may wish to consider a new addition to your prayer book and to your prayer life. Because Jesus taught his followers a new version of the *Shema* ("Hear O Israel! . . . Love God, love your neighbor . . .") and because the *Shema* was said at least two times a day in Jesus' time, you may also want to consider reciting the version Jesus taught every time you recite the Lord's Prayer. My own practice is to recite it with any prayer book I am using just before that prayer book asks us to recite the Lord's Prayer.

It was a mistake on the part of the Church to drop the customs of prayer it learned from Judaism. We are aware that such decisions were not official and were not universal, but somehow the sacred prayer traditions of Judaism were eliminated from the Church's own sacred tradition. So I am asking us to consider re-inserting Jesus' version of the Shema into our prayer books in order to remind ourselves of how Jesus taught that the entire Torah was to be understood: The will of God can be reduced to loving God and loving others.

◆

THE JESUS CREED

Hear O Israel! The Lord our God, the Lord is One. Love the Lord your God with all your heart, with all your soul, with all your mind, and with all your strength.

The second is this: Love your neighbor as yourself. There is no commandment greater than these.

NINTH, WE NEED HYMNS AND READINGS

The major prayer books include hymns. Both *The Liturgy of the Hours* and *The Book of Common Prayer* have a rich selection of hymns, and Phyllis Tickle has herself made an admirable and wide-ranging selection of hymns for her vespers prayers in *The Divine Hours*. I can't sing well, and I certainly don't know tunes by their names, but I can at least read the hymns aloud. When I know them, I sometimes sing them— sometimes Kris and I sing together the hymn in the vespers prayers.

The Church has always loved to sing, and some of its most creative people have created songs that the Church loves to sing still. Music has its way of taking words to their next level. Some have learned the sophisticated art of chanting the Psalter.

In addition to hymns, the Church has always advised Christians to read from the spiritual masters. There is nothing quite like *The Liturgy of the Hours* in its office of readings in any of the other prayer books. It contains pages of readings from the deep traditions of Christian spirituality. But those who don't use *The Liturgy of the Hours* have the opportunity and challenge to come up with their own devotional readings. I encourage you to choose the best paragraphs (maybe a page or two) of the best spiritual writings you know, and turn to them on a set basis for reminder and renewal. Or you may prefer to maintain a constant flow of classic spiritual books that you try to read for a few minutes every day. A good place to start your list is with Richard Foster's two books, *Devotional Classics* and *Spiritual Classics*.

AN INVITATION AND A PRAYER

I invite you to join me as I join others in praying, not simply alone *in* the church, but *with* the Church. I know that a commitment to praying with the Church is a challenge. But in the inconstancy of life, devotion to the hours of prayer provides us a quiet spot throughout each day. As we come to this quiet place, we may need to admit our resistance to the sacred tradition of praying the hours of prayer. But we may also confess that we know this tradition will fix our hearts on what matters most: loving God and loving others for the good of the world.

> O Almighty God,
> who alone canst order
> the unruly wills and affections of sinful men;
> Grant unto thy people,
> that they may love the thing which thou commandest,
> and desire that which thou dost promise;
> that so, among the sundry and manifold changes of the world,
> our hearts may surely there be fixed,
> where true joys are to be found;
> through Jesus Christ our Lord.
> Amen.

The Book of Common Prayer, the Collect for the Fourth Week after Easter

SOURCES

Sources are given once per chapter; page numbers refer to the pages quoted in the text anywhere in the chapter.

FRONTISPIECE

Orthodox Spirituality: An Outline of the Orthodox Ascetical and Mystical Tradition, by a Monk of the Eastern Church (2d ed.; Crestwood, NY: St. Vladimir's Seminary Press, 1996), 22.

CHAPTER 1

The Little Book of Hours: Praying with the Community of Jesus (Brewster, MA: Paraclete, 2003), ix, x. See **Mark Galli**, *Francis of Assisi and His World* (Oxford: Lion, 2002). For **Brother Lawrence**, *The Practice of the Presence of God* (Christian Classics; Brewster, MA: Paraclete, 1985), 93. On the prayer lives of pastors, I found information from the Keener Communications Group, July 2005.

CHAPTER 2

For **Abba Paul,** see B. Ward, ed., *The Wisdom of the Desert Fathers* (Oxford: Lion, 1998), 12. For **G. B. Caird**, see *New Testament Theology* (Oxford: Clarendon, 1994), 401.

CHAPTER 3

On **St. Macrina**, see Gregory of Nyssa, *The Life of Saint Macrina* (trans. K. Corrigan; Toronto: Peregrina, 2001), 39. On **Abraham Joshua Heschel**, see his *The Sabbath: Its Meaning for Modern Man* (New York: Farrar, Straus, Giroux, 1998), 3, 6.

CHAPTER 4

For the *Shema*, see L. A. Hoffman, ed., *The Sh'ma and Its Blessings* (My People's Prayer Book 1; (Woodstock, Vermont: Jewish Lights, 1997). On the *Ha-Tepillah or Amidah*, I have used the translation found in G. Vermes, M. Black, *The History of the Jewish People in the Age of Jesus Christ (175 BC–AD 135)* (4 vols.; ed. version of E. Schürer; Edinburgh: T & T Clark, 1979), 2.460. For **Joachim Jeremias**, see his *The Prayers of Jesus* (London: SCM, 1976), 74, from which I also take the following citation from Eliezer. For **Eliezer ben Hyrcanus**, see *Babylonian Talmud*, tractate *Berakot* 47b.

CHAPTER 5

On **Kathleen Norris**, see *Dakota: A Spiritual Geography* (Boston: Houghton Mifflin, 1993), 185-186. On **Esther de Waal**, *Seeking God: The Way of St. Benedict* (Collegeville, MN: The Liturgical Press, 2001), 149. On **Mark Roberts**, see *No Holds Barred: Wrestling with God in Prayer* (Nashville: Nelson, 2005), 4-5. For the story about **William Holladay**, see his *The Psalms through Three Thousand Years*, 154-155.

On **Luke Timothy Johnson**, see his *The Creed: What Christians Believe and Why it Matters* (New York: Doubleday, 2003), 5.

On **Jesus and prayer**, a good dictionary-length piece is James D. G. Dunn, "Prayer," in *The Dictionary of Jesus and the Gospels* (ed.

J. B. Green, S. McKnight, I. H. Marshall; Downers Grove, IL: IVP, 1992), 617–625. I quote from **G. B. Caird**, *New Testament Theology* (ed. L. D. Hurst; Oxford: Clarendon, 1994), 401. On **Mother Teresa**, see *Mother Teresa's Reaching Out in Love: Stories Told by Mother Teresa* (ed. E. Le Joly, J. Chaliha; New York: Barnes & Noble, 2002), 96-97.

CHAPTER 6

For the prayer by **Calvin**, see C. Manschreck, ed., *Prayers of the Reformers* (Philadelphia: Muhlenberg, 1958), 79. On **Robert Webber**, see his *Ancient-Future Time: Forming Spirituality through the Christian Year* (Grand Rapids, MI: Baker Books, 2004), 23, 33 (the prayer is adapted from *The Book of Common Prayer*). I have relied on his summaries for this section. For **Jonathan Hill**, see his *What Has Christianity Done for Us? How it shaped the world* (Downers Grove, IL: IVP, 2005), 40. On **Tertullian**, see his "The Chaplet, or *de Corona*," in The Ante-Nicene Fathers 3 (Grand Rapids, MI: Eerdmans, 1980), ch. 3 (p. 94).

CHAPTER 7

In general, for help with the Orthodox tradition, go to http://www.eighthdaybooks.com/ and you can use the "Contact Us" link.

On **Frederica Mathewes-Green**, see *Facing East: A Pilgrim's Journey into the Mysteries of Orthodoxy* (San Francisco: HarperSanFrancisco, 1997), 142-143. On **Alexander Schmemann**, *The Journals of Father Alexander Schmemann, 1973–1983* (trans. J. Schmemann; Crestwood, NY: St. Vladimir's Seminary

Press, 2000), 18, 71. **St. Augustine**: see in Lev Gillet, *The Jesus Prayer* (by a Monk of the Eastern Church; forew. K. Ware; Crestwood, NY: St. Vladimir's Seminary Press, 1997), 30. On **Tony Jones**, *The Sacred Way* (Grand Rapids, MI: Zondervan, 2005), 65. I have used the translation of Helen Bacovcin, *The Way of the Pilgrim and the Pilgrim Continues His Way* (New York: Image Doubleday, 2003). I do not find the second part, *The Pilgrim Continues His Way*, to be of much inspiration. I have used the four-volume edition of *The Philokalia* (ed. G. E .H. Palmer, P. Sherrard, K. Ware; London: Faber and Faber, 1979–1995). On **St. John of Climacus**, see L. Gillet, 39. I have quoted from **St. Simeon** from *The Way of the Pilgrim*, 10, and I have also quoted from p. 13. On the **Eastern Prayer book**, see *A Manual of Eastern Orthodox Prayers* (forew. A. Schmemann; explanatory notes by N. Zernov; Crestwood, NY: St. Vladimir's Seminary Press, 1983), x (for Zernov).

CHAPTER 8

On **Benedict's** *Rule*, for which there are many editions and publishers, I have used Norvene Vest, *Preferring Christ: A Devotional Commentary and Workbook on the* Rule of Saint Benedict (Trabuco Canyon, CA: Source Books, 2002), 1. The Rule of 1221 by Francis can be found in *The Writings of St. Francis* (Assisi: Edizioni Portiuncola, 1999), 65. For **Tony Jones**, see his *The Sacred Way: Spiritual Practices for Everyday Life* (Grand Rapids, MI: Zondervan, 2005), 122.

On **Flannery O'Connor**, see R. C. Wood, *Flannery O'Connor and the Christ-Haunted South* (Grand Rapids, MI: Eerdmans, 2004), 25. The Merton quotation is from Wood, p. 26 footnote #25. *The*

Habit of Being (ed. S. Fitzgerald; New York: Farrar, Straus & Giroux, 1979), 159, 422. On **Henri Nouwen**, I have taken material from Michael O'Laughlin, *God's Beloved: A Spiritual Biography of Henri Nouwen* (Maryknoll, NY: Orbis, 2004), 180, 181, 184. On the **Stations of the Cross**, see the introduction in .T. Jones, *The Sacred Way*, 135–147. On the **Glenstal Benedictine prayer book**, see *The Glenstal Book of Prayer: A Benedictine Prayer Book* (Collegeville, MN: Liturgical Press, 2001), 11, 13.

CHAPTER 9

On **David Adam**, Arthur Paul Boers, *The Rhythm of God's Grace* (Brewster, MA: Paraclete, 2003), 18. The quotation from **N. T. Wright** is from his book, *The Last Word* (San Francisco: HarperSanFrancisco, 2005), 131, 133.

On **Thomas Cranmer**, I have relied on Diarmaid MacCulloch, *Thomas Cranmer: A Life* (New Haven: Yale University Press, 1996). On **John Stott**, see Timothy Dudley-Smith, *John Stott: A Global Ministry. A Biography: The Later Years* (Downers Grove, IL: IVP, 2001), 450-451. On **C. S. Lewis**, I quote from Lyle Dorsett, *Seeking the Secret Place: The Spiritual Formation of C. S. Lewis* (Grand Rapids, MI: Brazos, 2004), 64.

CHAPTER 10

On **Phyllis Tickle**, I use her autobiography, *The Shaping of a Life* (New York: Doubleday, 2001), 36-37, 77. For **Arthur Paul Boers**, see his *The Rhythm of God's Grace* (Brewster, MA: Paraclete, 11, 13. For the poem of G. K. Chesterton, see M. Ward, *Gilbert Keith Chesterton* (New York: Sheed and Ward, 1943), 60.

CONCLUSION

The quotation from *The Little Book of Hours* is from p. ix. On **Margaret Silf**, see her *Sacred Spaces: Stations on a Celtic Way* (Brewster, MA: Paraclete, 2001), 9. On **Esther de Waal**, *Seeking God: The Way of St. Benedict* (Collegeville, MN: The Liturgical Press, 2001), 105. On **Ruth Haley Barton**, see her *Invitation to Solitude and Silence* (Downers Grove, IL: IVP, 2004), 29, 31. On the **Celtic dressing prayer**, I use it as found in de Waal, *Seeking God*, 96. On **Richard Foster**, see *Devotional Classics: Selected Readings for Individuals and Groups* (San Francisco: HarperSanFrancisco, 1993), and *Spiritual Classics: Selected Readings for Individuals and Groups on the Twelve Spiritual Disciplines* (San Francisco: HarperSanFrancisco, 2000).

AFTER WORDS

I am grateful again to the many who have read portions of this book or who have listened to my chatter about it. In particular, I am grateful to Kris, my lovely wife, who reads everything I write with a more-than-sympathetic ear but also a not-afraid-to-say this-is-boring ear. We have lived this book together in two ways: in prayer and in reading.

Also, I want to thank a singularly gifted student of mine, Renee Dinges, who read each chapter and gave both encouraging remarks and valuable suggestions. Renee has the ear of an editor and the heart of a pastor.

Many of the testimonials about using prayer books come from those who read my blog (www.jesuscreed.org). I am grateful to them for their permission to use their stories.

Others have commented on portions, including Bradley Nassif, Rob Merola, Trevin Wax, and Don Richmond.

Lil Copan edited this book in the week after the Chicago White Sox eliminated her Boston Red Sox from the 2005 Major League Playoffs. She was merciful to this Chicago dweller!

Once again, I cannot say enough about Paraclete Press and all the folks there who devote their lives to helping others learn to pray with the Church. Take this book as a gift from me to you.

Advent 2005

About Paraclete Press

Who We Are

Paraclete Press is an ecumenical publisher of books and recordings on Christian spirituality. Our publishing represents a full expression of Christian belief and practice—from Catholic to Evangelical, from Protestant to Orthodox.

Paraclete Press is the publishing arm of the Community of Jesus, an ecumenical monastic community in the Benedictine tradition. As such, we are uniquely positioned in the marketplace without connection to a large corporation and with informal relationships to many branches and denominations of faith.

We like it best when people buy our books from booksellers, our partners in successfully reaching as wide an audience as possible.

What We Are Doing

Books

Paraclete Press publishes books that show the richness and depth of what it means to be Christian. Although Benedictine spirituality is at the heart of all that we do, we publish books that reflect the Christian experience across many cultures, time periods, and houses of worship.

We publish books that nourish the vibrant life of the church and its people—books about spiritual practice, formation, history, ideas, and customs.

We have several different series of books within Paraclete Press, including the bestselling *Living Library* series of modernized classic texts; *A Voice from the Monastery*—giving voice to men and women monastics about what it means to live a spiritual life today; award winning literary faith fiction; and books that explore Judaism and Islam and discover how these faiths inform Christian thought and practice.

Recordings

From Gregorian chant to contemporary American choral works, our music recordings celebrate the richness of sacred choral music through the centuries. Paraclete is proud to distribute the recordings of the internationally acclaimed choir Gloriæ Dei Cantores, who have been praised for their "rapt and fathomless spiritual intensity" by *American Record Guide,* and the Gloriæ Dei Cantores Schola, which specializes in the study and performance of Gregorian chant. Paraclete is also the exclusive North American distributor of the Monastic Choir of St. Peter's Abbey in Solesmes, France, long considered to be a leading authority on Gregorian chant performance.

Learn more about us at our Web site:
www.paracletepress.com, or call us toll-free at
1-800-451-5006.

Also by Popular Evangelical Theologian,
Scot McKnight

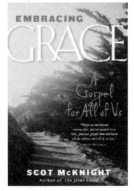

Embracing Grace

$16.95
Trade Paper, 182 pages
1-55725-453-2

Many preachers and teachers today reduce the gospel to forgiveness from sins and getting into heaven. But the message of the Bible is actually much bigger and better than just that. In *Embracing Grace*, Scot McKnight presents a more complete understanding of our relationship with Jesus that takes in the whole range of the biblical story.

"Helps us see beyond various flat, partial gospels to a rich, gracious gospel that embraces all the others, and all of us too."
—Brian McLaren

A Companion Guide to Embracing Grace

$6.95
Trade Paper, 84 pages
1-55725-483-4

This helpful "Companion Guide" will walk you through each chapter of *Embracing Grace* and make concrete suggestions of how to allow Christ's message to truly impact our lives, churches, and world more completely—as we seek the kingdom of God. Ideal for study groups.